A complete

Night
Magic

About the Author

Cassandra Eason is an international bestselling author and broadcaster on psychic and spiritual experience and folklore. She is the author of more than 40 titles and is regularly featured in the media. Other books by her include:

Aura Reading
Psychic Awareness
Cassandra Eason's Complete Book of Tarot
The Complete Book of Women's Wisdom
A Complete Guide to Divination
A Complete Guide to Psychic Development
10 Steps to Psychic Power
A Complete Guide to Magic and Ritual

CASSANDRA EASON

A complete guide to

Night
Magic

PIATKUS

Visit the Piatkus website!

Piatkus publishes a wide range of best-selling fiction and non-fiction, including books on health, mind, body & spirit, sex, self-help, cookery, biography and the paranormal.

If you want to:

- read descriptions of our popular titles
- buy our books over the Internet
- take advantage of our special offers
- enter our monthly competition
- learn more about your favourite Piatkus authors

VISIT OUR WEBSITE AT: **www.piatkus.co.uk**

© 2002 Cassandra Eason

First published in 2002 by
Judy Piatkus (Publishers) Ltd
5 Windmill Street, London W1T 2JA
email: info@piatkus.co.uk

The moral rights of the author have been asserted

A catalogue record for this book is available from the British Library

ISBN 0–7499–2361–X

Edited by Lizzie Hutchins
Artworks by Rodney Paull

Set by Phoenix Photosetting, Chatham, Kent
Printed and Bound in Great Britain by
Butler & Tanner Ltd, Frome, Somerset

To Ginny

Contents

Introduction

Who will walk into the darkness with me?

The call of the Crone Goddess from the author's personal
Book of Shadows

Darkness and night are often associated in myth and popular fantasy with evil, negativity, ghosts and black witchcraft. So many people fear the dark and draw the curtains when the light fades. In the modern world, we work in buildings with constant heat and light that turn winter into summer, night into day. We live in an unremitting whirl of constant activity with none of the ebbs that are necessary if we are to live in harmony with the flow of our natural cycles.

Darkness is an intrinsic part of these cycles. Half of the world is in darkness while the other is in light and for part of the year the night is longer than the day. Two of the seasons are dark ones, autumn and winter, with their own dark deities and special energies for transformation, regeneration and spiritual growth. Without darkness we would not appreciate the light and without the nurturing, restorative powers of the night there would be no daily rebirth with the dawn.

In many creation myths, the universe begins with darkness, sometimes called the Void, the Abyss or Chaos. However, in Buddhism this darkness is regarded as clear light. It is the source and material that enables the universe to evolve and grow. It may be that the divine spark uses this potential, this dark jewel, to create and increase opportunity and creativity in our lives. Our soul itself may be like the *yin/yang* sign, a balance of darkness and light, each part containing the seed of the other.

Yin and yang symbol

This book works with these natural rhythms of light and dark. By weaving ritual in the darkness, we can discover that darkness and light are equally creative and empowering. We will tap, too, into the energies of the dark seasons to strengthen our inner world and to allow ideas and plans to lie fallow in order to emerge naturally in the spring.

When we work with the darkness, we are not leaving behind our divine spark of light but rather bringing together the two aspects of ourselves, dark and light. Initially, because we may be unused to exploring our inner caverns, we may need to spend a great deal of time working with the night energies to redress the balance and reclaim our wise old soul.

The path of the night is an exciting one, where like the shamans and magicians of old you can explore your dreams and walk in dark or starry places. As you work with night energies, you will rediscover the psychic powers you perhaps last used freely in childhood, when possibility was limited only by your own imagination.

The powers of the night will both fill you with energy for the coming day and set you back in tune with the natural rhythms of your body, the Earth and the Moon. By slowing to the gentle rhythms of the night, you can regenerate your physical and psychic batteries. You will be able to access the wise unconscious parts of yourself and to explore the past, the future and the lands of mythology. Freed of daytime constraints, you can use your mind or, as some people believe, the spirit body we have within our physical body to travel to other realms.

You will need to leave all your maps and expectations behind, for this is a journey into the unknown. You are limited only by the extent of your own imaginative faculties, for the night is a realm where the imagination rules.

The Otherworld of Night

At night the constraints of the day are replaced by a dark seamless mantle glittering with stars, bathed in moonlight or illuminated with dancing candles. Our minds are free to kick off the cumbersome clothing of the workaday world and roam through the lands of faery under the hill, the midnight mountains with their ethereal mysterious earth lights, forests so thick it is always perpetual night, crypts, tunnels and other places of mystery.

The night is also filled with benign spirits and sources of power. Most angelic visitations occur after dark. Devas and nature spirits that care for natural places may be heard and felt in the stillness of the countryside at twilight.

Ghosts, too, walk more freely in the night air when the barriers of this world merge with adjoining dimensions. These are not the fearsome spectres of horror films but apparitions or impressions left on places such as battlegrounds that are imprinted with strong emotion, or areas where natural earth energies converge and give power to fuel spirit forms left from the past.

The majority of ghosts, however, are known to those who see, hear or sense their presence. They may be spirits who return because of unfinished business with the living, perhaps to put right a quarrel or to peep lovingly into the cot of a newborn baby. The smell of a grandmother's favourite perfume as we wake from a dream of her is not spooky but deeply reassuring and suggests that love and our essential spirit can survive the grave.

Darkness, too, has always been the time for magical ritual, a time when our mysterious powerful alter ego supersedes the conscious rational mind. Our unconscious self can use the energies of the night to empower symbols and thought forms, bringing wishes to manifestation when morning breaks.

Sleep also unlocks the messages of the subconscious, enabling us to discover our true selves. Meditation is easier too after dark, whether you are an expert or are new to the art. Later I describe meditating in detail (*see pages 21–3*). But in essence if you sit by a moonlit pool, look on to a darkened garden when the household is asleep, gaze up at the stars or sit in a quiet green place where it is always twilight, you will need no technique. You mind will move quite spontaneously to inner stillness and the everyday world will recede, leaving you connected to the very centre of silence.

Using This Book

In this book each chapter introduces a particular area of night or winter energy. It shows how your own buried powers can be explored within the constraints of a busy life to bring increased harmony and spiritual awareness. We will use a variety of techniques – rituals, meditations, visualisations, divination and most of all exploring quiet places and the kingdom of the Earth and the sky at night. Each is a different way of attaining knowledge of night powers.

Though I have used examples of dark magical places from different parts of the world, you can find similar sites that are close to your home or that you can visit during a weekend away. The emphasis is on creating inner magical settings and on working with your own night altar that you can create in a quiet recess of your home or garden.

Some methods will be helpful, others less so, and as you work, you will devise your own patterns and rituals as well as places that become your night sanctuaries. If you are an insomniac or fear the dark, these problems will disappear over the weeks and months. Thus you can pass on to the next generation the joys and wonders of the world when the light fades.

Learning to use your own reawakened inner wisdom will help you to evolve spiritually and to take the stillness and harmony you have gained back into your daily world. You will become more intuitive and less influenced by the mood swings of others and by external situations, an oasis of calm in a frantic world.

Moving into Night Mode

When you have time, spend a weekend or a few days in the countryside, either camping or staying in a cottage or chalet. Watch the night sky undisturbed by the light pollution of towns and listen to the cries of the night creatures and the scurrying animals that make the night their own. Live by the natural light cycle, going to bed when your candle has burned through and waking with the dawn. You will be amazed at the restorative effect this can have, even in a weekend.

Try also to synchronise with the prevailing energies of the Moon (*see pages 41–5*) and you and those with whom you interact will benefit from increased tranquillity and serenity.

The more experience you have of the night, the easier it will be to access your own dark inner places and simply by closing your eyes bring calm to the most frantic daytime moment.

Walk through the shadowy doorway into your inner treasure house of intuition, insight and as yet untapped psychic awareness. Take your first step into the darkness and welcome its positive powers . . .

1

Beginning Night Magic

To enter into the world of the night and discover its riches, first attune yourself to the darkness.

Learning to Love the Darkness

- Wait until it is dark, draw the curtains and close the door so no light can enter.

- Light five white candles in a horseshoe shape around a bowl of clear water.

- Look at the candles reflected in the water. Allow images or thoughts to come and go. Do not force them. The images may initially appear within your mind, stimulated by the pattern of the candles on the dark water. This is one of the oldest forms of divination (*see pages 155–6*).

- Now blow out one of the candles and look again at the water. You will find that the imagery is more vivid, not less, as your unconscious mind compensates for the loss of light.

- Continue extinguishing candles and gazing into the progressively darkened water until only one candle is burning. Your night-imaging powers will make the visions increasingly richer.

- Close your eyes and visualise the water with the light on it. Allow images to form in the visualised water.

- Open your eyes and while gazing into the actual dark water, continue the imaging process.

- When you are ready, blow out the final candle and look into the dark water for the final time, allowing the images from your inner world to appear on the surface.

Allow your imagination to roam free in these early stages, nudging it if necessary, until the process becomes unconscious. Your psyche will soon kick in. As your eyes adjust, you will find that the water is no longer inky black but has paler areas. You may become aware of the colours of the night – rich ruby reds, midnight blues, amethyst and rich green, silver and burnished gold (*see also page 16*).

You are cocooned in this special place and could, if you wished, travel through the night to dream planes and places, to caves, deep dark woods or the dimness at the bottom of the sea. Oriental wisdom describes *yin*, the dark element, as a seamless cloak; so it is that darkness can remove all the barriers and conscious restrictions that keep us firmly in our own space and time.

- Trace the shape of a doorway in the dark water with the index finger of your power hand – the one you write with – and visualise it opening, if you wish, giving you a glimpse of another world. You will not see anything frightening, though sometimes we can create our own demons of the night from our fears, but these will dissolve if we touch them.

- When you are ready, open the curtains or the door and let the light return.

You can work with your dark portal at any time, not only for divinatory purposes but also for settling yourself after the world has been particularly brash or intrusive.

Preparing Your Night Place

You can, of course, work anywhere. However, night magic is enriched by setting aside a quiet place in your home where you can build up a repository of the gentle night power through your rituals, divination and meditations. Here you can keep your special night crystals, candles, incense and tools, and carry out rituals alone or with trusted friends or family. You can meditate, send and receive healing and develop your prophetic voice.

If you live in an area where there is bright street lighting, you may wish to put heavy dark curtains at the window and perhaps over the door to mark your space.

Even if you work in your bedroom in a shared flat or a busy family household, it is possible, with a little reorganisation of priorities, as well as furniture, to claim a special space. There may be a garden shed that is used for clutter. The children may have a den or family room for watching television, or there may be an attic or basement that could be appropriated. DIY stores often sell self-assemble garden chalets that do not need either planning permission or much space and are wonderful for night work as you can overlook the garden through large windows.

When it is warm enough, work outdoors. Bushes or plants in tubs can make a screen to give you privacy and create a circle from which you can look upwards at the stars in your roofless temple. In an apartment, you could adapt a balcony or roof terrace. From your open place you can watch the constellations wheel round and each day see the Moon rise in a different place in the sky.

Whenever possible, spend a few minutes at night or just before dawn outdoors. Fill your lungs with the crisp night air, the clear light of the Buddhists (*see pages 17–18*). At twilight, too, make a quiet moment to focus on the darkening sky to restore inner harmony. If possible, play truant for a brief time from the cares and responsibilities of everyday life and slip outdoors, away from noise and lighting, and allow yourself to merge with the healing twilight.

Making Your Night Altar

The word 'altar' should not summon up any eerie impressions. You are not setting up anything dangerous or unholy, but a small working area. It need be no more than a small table or thick square of slate resting on bricks that you can push under the bed during the day to create space. Alternatively, leave it ready, as I do, covered with dark silk or a spangled cloth during the daylight.

You can keep your night magic tools (*see below*) in a box ready for use on the altar. However, there is no harm in letting daylight touch the altar, for light is the twin of darkness. Indeed, some practitioners do leave the altar set with two candles, a focal crystal and perhaps fresh flowers all day to absorb the light power. It is your choice.

You may prefer an altar that is about waist height so that you can stand in front of it, or a lower coffee-table type so that you can sit on the floor. Some people have both and carry the low one outside for garden work.

If possible, place the altar so that you can face North as you work, as this is the direction of the Earth element, midnight and winter. If this is not possible, you can use a symbolic North and set the other directions at 90 degree angles to it.

You should be able to move all around the altar to create a protective circle in ritual.

If there is a window in the room, position your altar so that on moonlit nights when you draw back the curtain, the light will shine on any water and crystals.

You do not need a black cloth. Choose one that symbolises the richness of the night – silver, midnight blue or ruby red – perhaps decorated with stars or moons.

The Tools of Night Magic

- You will need a silver or clear crystal bowl to fill with water for divination and for ritual. It need not be large but should be deep. Keep this in the West (actual or symbolic) of your altar to represent the ancient element of Water and the direction of dusk and autumn.

- A small open silver or crystal dish will hold salt for blessing and protective work. Salt is a naturally cleansing and protective substance and will absorb negative energies. Use sea salt and keep your main supply in a lidded jar to keep it dry, then fill your dish just before a ritual. Place the salt in the North as the substance of Earth.

- You can also set a small silver or crystal bell in the North. This is sometimes rung in the four directions to begin rituals.

- Represent the Fire element with a candle in the South, the direction of noon and summer. This candle, which is generally lit during more formal rituals, is usually burnished gold or deep red.

- Set incense in the East for the element of Air, dawn and spring.

By using night magic colours and fragrances you can maintain the emphasis on the power of the night.

Night Candle Colours

Candles are important in night rituals for opening and closing the ritual, for adding the power of Fire symbolically to an object that is being empowered and for sending healing light.

Choose dark red, silver, rich dark green, deep purple, midnight blue and burnished gold.

Night Incenses and Oils

Incense has traditionally been used to endow protective or empowering properties through the fragrance chosen, to represent the ancient element of Air and to cleanse or mark a ritual space.

Good night incenses are jasmine, patchouli, pine, sandalwood, myrrh, mimosa and rose.

Night Crystals

Crystals are valuable in ritual and in healing because they contain energies that can be transmitted for positive purposes to people, animals, plants and places.

Good night crystals are Apache tears/obsidian, angelite/celestite, smoky quartz, purple and green fluorite rutilated quartz, jet, blue beryl, rose quartz, moonstone/selenite, garnet, jade, pearl, opal, onyx, sodalite and dark agates. Their protective and healing properties have been recognised since the time of ancient Egypt and have been used by many cultures.

These crystals are also effective as a focus for psychic insights in the form of images seen within the crystal or stimulated by the reflective surface. This technique is known as scrying. Especially powerful are deep blue beryl, amethyst or purple fluorite. Or you can use an uncut piece of amethyst or an amethyst geode. Amethyst is the single most healing and protective night stone and need not be expensive if you use the unpolished kind.

Your Focal Crystal

In the centre of your night altar set a large dark crystal sphere, either in front of or as a substitute for a statue. You will use this as a focus for night breathing and meditation, night healing and scrying.

A Crystal Wand

This can help you to direct energies, especially in healing. It need not be long but should be pointed at one end and made of a dark crystal. You can often buy a smoky quartz crystal point quite cheaply. You can use your crystal wand for casting circles in formal rituals, for stirring salt into water to create circles of protection and also for directing healing rays.

Alternatively, use a paper knife made of silver, the metal of the night. I have one bearing the image of owl, an archetypal creature of the night, engraved on the handle. You can also improvise with a long pointed twig from a moon tree, such as alder, sycamore or willow.

A Crystal Pendulum

One of my most valuable tools for day or night magic is a crystal pendulum. This can aid you in decision-making and by its positive or negative swing express physically what your inner wisdom is telling you. It can also be used for clearing energy blockages in the body or even a place, in healing and in detecting when paranormal energies are present.

You can buy amethyst or rose quartz pendulums that are especially potent for night magic.

The Book of Shadows

Magical workbooks are traditionally called Books of Shadows, partly because magic has been mainly practised at night. You can create your own book for night magic, which can be as elaborate or plain as you wish, because the rituals and experiences you record are essentially personal and reflect your innermost self. You might like to buy a plain loose-leafed book with a spangled or velvet cover or a rich leather-bound type. You could even record your notes on a computer and print them out to put in a binder. Even though we are accessing ancient wisdom, there is no reason to turn our backs on technology. A Book of Shadows, of whatever kind, is a treasure you create and may hand on one day as a precious inheritance.

Keep your night magic book on your altar as you work, though you may wish to put it in a drawer or locked cupboard if other people have access to your mystical workspace.

It can be incredibly therapeutic to write up your book with a proper pen and coloured inks before bed. You can list rituals you have devised or carried out, the results of divination and those combinations of herbs, incense and oils you find helpful in healing or meditation.

One part of the journal can form an almanac, listing significant days for a month or two ahead. Consult an astrological diary or printed almanac that notes the movements of the Sun, Moon and planets so that you can time your rituals accordingly (*see pages 50–9 and 81–7*).

In another section that you might label 'Oracles', record any channelling or prophecy you receive as a result of working with specific constellations or in dark natural places.

Have a place to retell your favourite myths about night, winter and lunar deities as well as the various star formations. Feel free to write a new ending or to introduce characters, as myths are essentially a living tradition.

Make a healing section in which you can write the names of people, animals or places that need help. Open the book at this section on your altar when you light the candles so the healing light shines on the names. At other times you can keep your book closed on the altar.

The Cloak of Night

You can wear absolutely anything for night magic. While you are tramping around outdoors or star watching, you may be most comfortable in jeans and a warm coat. However, for indoor and for private outdoor work, you could buy or make a star-spangled robe (in a basic kaftan design without trailing hems or sleeves if you are working with candles) that you keep especially for night magic.

You may also find a light cloak is helpful to wrap around you when sitting outdoors or to mark your enclosed space in meditation. It will also make an impromptu altar space for crystals and artefacts if you are away from home.

Preparing the Altar

Position the candles to the left and right of the centre of the altar.

In the centre of the altar, some people place a statue of one of the Moon or winter deities in dark wood or stone. You can get some beautiful Egyptian figurines or a Black Madonna and child, the Virgin Mary in her winter aspect modelled on the Egyptian Isis and her son Horus. Circle this with your favourite small dark crystals.

Alternatively, you may prefer to have a vase of white flowers, the colour of the Moon, as your focus, or a large crystal.

Preparing Yourself for Night Magic

In the daytime, we sometimes rush preparations. With night magic you can take longer.

To work your magic, you might like to have a quick light supper and work in the twilight or stay up later or get up earlier, just before dawn. One time may seem especially right for you, either because it fits in with your lifestyle or because your personal psychic energies are especially strong then.

Ritual baths are common in many cultures before spiritual work. For night magic, try the following:

- At night-time, dusk or before dawn, fill your bathroom with tiny night-lights or dusky pink candles that cast pools of radiance in the bathwater.

- Add a few drops of ylang ylang, rose or lavender essential oil to the water or float a net with dried lavender flowers or rose petals in the bath.

- This is your time for washing away the cares and anxieties of the day, so make it a significant occasion, even if you have only ten minutes. Use water that is warm but not too hot.

- Play gentle background music and visualise yourself floating on

dark water through the light pools or on a gentle sea tinged by
moonlight.

• When you are ready, get out and swirl the light pools as you take
out the plug. In this way the daytime tensions are carried away.
Whisper '*Go in peace, sorrow cease*' over and over until the bath is
empty.

• Alternatively, you can take a ritual shower using essential oil
shower gel and visualising yourself standing under a waterfall in
moonlight.

• Dress slowly; brush your hair rhythmically and then, carrying
one of the candles (extinguish the others), go to your altar.

Working with Your Night Altar

Sometimes you will want just to light your candles and incense and
sit in front of the altar. It can be very therapeutic to hold the focal
crystal or one of your other crystals and allow your psyche to direct
your thoughts and actions.

At other times, you may weave rituals either for specific purposes
or to open yourself to the deep wisdom of the dark. You may gaze
into the water in your bowl, illuminated by candlelight or the
Moon, and allow words or images to flow on the water and in your
mind.

Quiet times are just as valuable as specific ritual.

Some weeks you may work with your altar several times. But if
everyday life becomes frantic, you might do no more than light a
candle for a week or more. However, the magic will not go away
and in time you will value your night place as a resource for
strengthening your everyday world.

To begin with, familiarise yourself with the energies of the night,
then later you can perform a ritual to dedicate your altar.

Protection

In the next chapter I describe in detail methods of psychic protection for you and your loved ones. These will help you to overcome

fears and to repel any malice, whether from an earthly source or from free-floating negativity.

If you carry out rituals only with positive intent and do not practise magic when you are angry, anxious or exhausted, you are protected from any possible harm.

However, on occasions you may wish to include a simple but effective shielding technique in your preparations for a prolonged or emotionally charged ritual. It can also be helpful before divination, especially if you are reading for someone who may be unhappy or angry.

You can also use this method at any time you are subject to fears or dangers of the night. Or you can protect a loved one who is away for the night or travelling in a potentially hazardous place or in a risky situation.

Setting Up a Protective Shield

- Sit in your special night place or wherever you are working.

- Clear your mind by visualising a jug of dark water being emptied into a deep silent pool. Or imagine stars in a clear night sky fading one by one, leaving only velvet blackness.

- Holding a semi-transparent dark crystal, such as a smoky quartz or clear amethyst, begin a slow breathing pattern. Visualise yourself inhaling the crystalline light through your nose and slowly exhale any jagged red strands of tension, fear or worry through your mouth as a prolonged sigh.

- As you breathe, see the purple or smoky grey crystal enclosing you, your night place or a loved one in a protective shield that surrounds you but through which you can see quite clearly.

- Ask your special guardian or one of the dark protective angels to watch over you and keep you or your family member safe from harm.

- When you finish the ritual or when the darkness is past, you can visualise the crystalline shield of light fading, leaving you quiet and at peace. Thank any guardians you asked for protection and bid them farewell. They will not leave you entirely but will retreat to a distance until you seek further active protection.

Making a Protective Circle

For less formal rituals, you can visualise a crystalline circle of protection or a ring of protective fire around you and your altar. A protective circle marks out a space which negative energies or thoughts cannot enter.

- For more formal or protracted work, use a dark pointed crystal or paper knife to draw a circle of crystalline or silver light waist-high in the air, beginning in the North. Alternatively, you can create a circle of smoke with a lighted sage smudge or incense stick.

- Outdoors, you can draw your circle clockwise in earth or sand or form one from stones or shells. Make it large enough to sit in and walk around.

- Though the direction of night is Moon-wise or anti-clockwise (this is because although the Moon travels through the sky from left to right, like the hands of the clock, it waxes and wanes from right to left), you may still prefer to cast your circle clockwise. You are not summoning up any negative powers if you make a Moon-wise circle. It is your choice. But since magic generally works clockwise, it can save worrying about reversing elements, directions, etc.

- Afterwards, you can uncast your crystal or earth circle by walking around it Moon-wise. Smoke circles do not need uncasting.

- Before ending the ritual, or as you uncast the circle, you may wish to say: 'May the circle that is cast remain unbroken in our hearts and in our lives. Blessed be.' That way you can carry away into your life the protection of the sacred space.

The Night Rainbow

We think of the night as black. But once you become familiar with using it magically, you may become aware of its essential colours. You may see deep inky blues, smoky greys, ruby red, rich deep emerald, amethyst and silver, even faint burnished gold. These are the colours I and a number of people I have taught see. However, you may see even more colours or develop an alternative night rainbow. If so, note them in your Book of Shadows.

Seeing the Night Rainbow

- At first you may need to visualise the colours as spheres of light dancing over the altar.

- Light your night candles, beginning with your favourite colour and adding one more colour each night.

- Sit by the light for about five minutes, on consecutive nights if possible, visualising the colour(s) extending as a halo around the flame.

- On the night of the seventh candle, you will have all the colours glowing before you. Half-close your eyes and the colours will merge and dance.

- As you extinguish the candles, imagine the colours merging into your night rainbow.

- On the eighth night, light only the first colour you chose. Picture the other colours emerging from the darkness.

- If you persevere, if necessary repeating the eight-night cycle, in time you will see your night rainbow spontaneously whenever you enter your special place or work outdoors.

Learning to Breathe like a Creature of the Night

To attune yourself to the energies of the night, especially if thoughts of the day intrude, you can begin your sessions by practising night breathing. Pure night air is like the breeze on a mountain top at midnight or a moonlit waterfall that can clear away all the litter and clutter of our psyche, leaving stillness and purity.

Though we may think of the life force, called *prana* in Hindu philosophy and *ch'i* in the Oriental, in terms of light, night-time *prana* is like a clear stream of flowing black ice or a dark transparent crystalline stream. You can draw this *prana* not only from the night sky but also upwards from the dark earth if you stand on grass or in an old place with stones, from the sea when dusk has fallen and from trees in dark woodlands.

If you are working indoors, draw the curtains if your room overlooks street lighting, but leave the window open.

Alternatively, work with your outdoor altar. This can be as formal or informal as you like – a tree stump, a large rock or a picnic table in a secluded spot.

Do this exercise before lighting the altar candles.

Night Breathing Method

- Begin by visualising yourself filled with white protective light.

- Focus on a point in the darkness directly ahead.

- As you look, the sphere will cease to be pure black but may assume one of the colours of the night, perhaps initially purple or blue.

- Begin by taking a slow deep breath through your nose, counting one and two and three. Hold your breath for one and two and three, and then exhale to the same rhythm. Then pause for the same time interval before inhaling again.

- Concentrate on creating a regular pattern so that you merge with the darkness and breathe in time with the pulse of the universe. You will hear this as if you are sitting in the centre of a ticking clock once your rhythm is established.

- Keep your eyes open and still focused on the point.

- Visualise yourself flowing as part of this dark life stream. Feel every pore of your body breathing in harmony with the ticking of the clock and the slow-flowing water.

- As you lose identity with your physical body, you lose its limitations and may find yourself travelling in your mind to other places in the world, to the past and future or to the realms of myth. In later chapters we will work more with travelling the 'night steed'. But for now accept such images that come spontaneously and enjoy the sensation of being one with the universe.

- After a while, you will become aware of your breathing again and you will begin to feel the boundaries of the physical world and your separate self returning.

Though the exercise may only have occupied five or ten minutes of earthly time, you may feel as though you are waking from a deep sleep or returning from a long journey. This can be a good way of restoring your harmony with the world even if you do not go on to other rituals or night work.

Using Night Breathing for Manipulating Thought Forms

One of the most valuable ways of using night breathing is to create the backdrop or canvas for any visualisation work. This may be for healing or for drawing strengths to you or even material things or better conditions at work or home.

In night magic, as in all magic, when you begin manipulating energies very moral rules apply. For with increased personal power comes responsibility. You can only ever work with positive purpose, for whatever you send out in the way of energies will return to you threefold.

You can ask for enough for your needs and a little more. This means no enormous lottery wins, but maybe a windfall big enough to pay an unexpected bill or to help friends or family. Then, later, when you have surplus time and energy, you can repay the cosmos by offering practical support to a person, creature or place in need.

It is important that magic is used for the benefit of others, but sometimes you do need to get yourself on track first. Sometimes you have to ask for something specific on which your survival depends. If possible, however, leave precise details to the universe, which may be more imaginative in its gift to you. What we want and what we need can be different.

Asking for Help or Healing

- Once you have established a rhythm with your breathing, picture what it is you need or the person you want to help or heal in the dark sphere on which you are focusing. At first the image will be quite small and shadowy, as it is drawn from the dark sea of potential within you.

- Increase the size of the image and the clarity, as though you are controlling a giant cinema screen, so that it fills your field of vision, while maintaining your breathing rhythm so that the build-up is gradual and smooth.

- When the image has reached full size and clarity in your mind, create a sudden explosion of visualised light, as though capturing the image in a camera flash or on X-ray film. This will momentarily illuminate the blackness with brilliant contrasting whiteness as thought is given birth.

- The light fades as fast as it came as you slowly return to merge with the darkness and finally return to the everyday world. The healing will have reached its source.

If you were focusing on a specific need, your dreams may be filled with ideas of how you can realise it in your daily life.

The next morning, use the accumulated energy to take the first step, however small, to making the wish happen.

Repeat the ritual weekly if necessary, each time taking more small steps.

Encountering Your Night Guardian

As you work with night magic, you may gradually become aware of a guardian who never intrudes but hovers close by. They will enfold you in protection and in time interpret prophetic messages for you. Each person sees their personal night guardian in different ways. It may be the guardian angel or spirit who appeared in our dreams when we were children.

If you go to an art gallery containing works from the Renaissance to the beginning of the 20th century, you will see paintings in which even angels and Archangels associated with light such as Michael and the healing angel Raphael are clothed in the colours of the night – opulent plum red, burnished gold, dark velvet green, midnight blue and royal purple. You may have one of these splendid angelic guides protecting you.

Alternatively, you may meet an altogether more muted though no less powerful guardian, perhaps a shadowy brown or grey figure, a wise hermit or ancient sage, a nun or a priestess. You may meet them in your dreams not long after you begin your night magic work. You may first become aware of them in the flame of a dark candle or the glitter of a crystal as you sit quietly before your night altar. Perhaps the first meeting will be at an old stone circle or on a hillside in the twilight. These guardians are not ghosts, rather the essences of wise teachers who may never have lived on Earth but choose to teach humankind.

Some believe that the guardian is the evolved part of your soul that your mind projects as a separate entity. You cannot access this evolved self consciously, but it becomes clearer and more vocal at night, when the 'younger brother' conscious mind is not demanding all the attention and bright light is not blurring your clairvoyant vision.

Seeking Out Your Night Guardian

- If after a few weeks of night magic you have not become aware of your guardian, find a white or light-coloured wall. When darkness falls, light a large white pillar candle so that it casts shadows on the wall.

- Open a window or use a small electric fan so that the flame dances.

- Through half-closed eyes, focus on the shadows and you will see the outline of your guardian.

- Now transfer your gaze to the actual flame and allow an image to build up. Do not force it. Close your eyes, open them, blink, stare hard at the flame and you will glimpse your guardian, either in the flame or in the halo around it.

- When you return your gaze to the shadows, you may be rewarded with a longer vision.

- If the images appear in your mind's eye, that is just as significant. You may hear words with your clairaudient or inner ear, perhaps a message of guidance. Alternatively, you may be filled with a sense of peace and the knowledge that you are protected.

Night Meditation

Just before dawn and just after dusk are traditionally times when night meditation is most easily practised, as you can flow with the energies of the transition between day and night (*see also pages 192–4*).

Night meditation is slower and gentler than daytime work and may follow on naturally from night breathing. You can also use meditation as a prelude to a ritual as a way of opening your psychic channels.

Centring Your Mind on the Silence of the Night

- In your special place, light a deep blue candle directly behind your focal crystal so that the light shines directly on it.

- Next to the candle, light an incense stick in jasmine or sandalwood and allow the smoke to curl over the crystal.

- The smoke will form the focus of your night meditation, inter-playing with crystal and candlelight.

- If you are unfamiliar with meditation, it may be helpful to play soft music – pan pipes, harp music or synthesised pieces with perhaps wolf or dolphin sounds flowing through them.

- Begin night breathing, but do not count breaths. Instead, allow your breath to find its own pattern. This will naturally slow as you relax into the meditation.

- Recite a simple continuous mantra either aloud or in your mind – 'I am the Night, the Night is within me and around, surrounds' – and let it gradually slow down and fade into silence. Silence is said to be the most perfect sound of all.

- Hold the smoke image constant through half-closed eyes and, if you wish, after a while close your eyes. Etch the image of the smoke, crystal and candle on the inner screen of your mind. In essence, you are emptying the mind of clutter by filling it with the smoke image.

- You may receive impressions or hear words, but do not attempt to hold on to them or analyse them, just let them flow on the smoke stream.

- In time you will become aware of the focus receding. Do not be in too much of a hurry to return to the everyday world.

- Open your eyes but remain still. Allow the images or impressions to flow once more through your mind as you watch the smoke. Record any that seem significant in your Book of Shadows.

In subsequent meditations you can change the focus. A water feature trickling in total darkness is one of my favourites. As you become more experienced, try sitting in total darkness while focusing on an inner image of moonlight on water or the stars in the sky.

Your First Night Magic Ritual

You can carry out your first formal night magic ritual at any time during the Moon's cycle. If there is a choice, begin as the Moon waxes, a few days before the full Moon, so that you are filled naturally with enthusiasm and positivity (*see page 52*).

To prepare for this ritual, leave pure spring or mineral water exposed to the Sun and Moon for a full 24 hours, beginning at dusk.

Before you begin, put the phone on silent answer and turn off all faxes.

Dedicating Your Altar and Your Work

- Check your altar is ready, perhaps with fresh flowers of a rich deep colour or white for the Moon. Make sure also you have the mundane items such as tapers and matches.

- You will need to fill a small dish or bowl with water as well as the larger one. Set this small bowl in the West next to the large bowl. Use the water that you have left exposed to a Sun and Moon cycle, as this is a special ritual.

- Sit or stand before the altar and light your altar candles, the candle of the South and the incense.

- Some people have a special secret name for ritual, perhaps that of one of the deities of the Moon or night (*see pages 42–5 for suggestions*) or an angelic name, that of a favourite star or constellation or even a night power animal with whose qualities you identify (*see pages 163–5*). You may refer to yourself by your usual or your magical name in ritual.

- Holding your special crystal, create your sphere of protective crystalline light around you and the altar. As you do so, ask mentally that you may be protected and declare that you work only with the highest intent and for the greatest good.

- If there is a special angel or deity you revere, or you have encountered your guardian, even if you do not yet know their name, ask them to guide you. Alternatively, you can ask the more abstract benign powers of darkness and the night to protect you as you work.

- As this is a special occasion, create a triple circle around yourself and the altar, using all four of the ancient elements as follows.

- Add a pinch of salt to the small dish of water, stirring it clockwise three times with a dark pointed crystal. Now moving around the altar, beginning in the North, sprinkle a circle of saltwater, saying: 'I cast my night circle, asking the power and protection of Earth and Water. Blessings be.'

- Next, take a lighted incense stick or smudge stick and cast a second clockwise circle over the first, again beginning in the North, saying: 'I cast my night circle, asking the power and protection of Air. Blessings be.'

- Finally, carry a deep purple candle around the same circle saying: 'I cast my night circle asking the power and protection of Fire. Blessings be.'

- Walk around the circle clockwise, ringing your silver bell at the four main directions and saying in turn: 'May there be peace and sanctity in the North/East/South/West.'

- When you have completed the circle, return the bell to the altar.

- Next, you are going to bless the four directions. Walk directly from the altar to the chosen direction and then complete the circuit by walking around the outside of the circle with the elemental substance of the direction (salt for the North, incense for the East, fire for the South and water for the West) before returning in a straight path to the altar.

- Take the dish of salt and, going to the North, face outwards, hold it high and say: 'Night guardian of the North, I welcome you with salt and ask that you bless my altar and my work.'

- Stand for a few moments. Visualise mists clearing and the guardian of the North standing sentinel. It may be an angel or an altogether different kind of being. We all see these guardian powers in different ways.

- Return the salt to the altar and carry the lighted incense to the East. Facing outwards, create an arc shoulder-high in smoke and say: 'Night guardian of the East, I welcome you with incense and ask that you bless my altar and my work.'

- Allow the guardian of the East to take form in your mind's eye.

- Return the incense to the altar and take the candle from the altar. Carry it to the South, face outwards, make an arc of fire and say: 'Night guardian of the South, I welcome you with fire and ask that you bless my altar and my work.'

- Visualise your guardian of the South.

- Return the candle to the altar and pick up the larger bowl of water. Carry it to the West, welcome the guardian of the West and ask for blessings on the altar and work. Sprinkle a few drops of water on the ground as you face the West and wait for this guardian to appear.

- Do not return the water to the West, but place it in the centre of the altar. In it you are going to focus the powers of the night.

- Taking the altar candles, hold them in a cross pattern over the water – being careful that no hot wax drips on you – and ask the positive powers of the night to enter the candles and the flame within you so that you may use your abilities for healing and for doing good to the world and to all its creatures.

- Make your own personal dedication. You may see your night rainbow arched overhead, shafts of starlight and moonlight or a transparent dark light entering the candle flames.

- When you have finished, say: 'Flame and flare, darkness and light, fire and water are one.'

- As you say the last word, plunge the wicks into the bowl and with a hiss the flames will be extinguished. (Never pour water over burning candles, as this will cause them to burn even more fiercely. Cut off the source of air instead with a metal container.)

- Place the extinguished candles back in their holders and sit quietly in the light of the single burning candle, gazing into the water, where you may see images cast from your mind or hear words from one of the guardians.

- Touch the night power water with your index finger, making a circle on the surface. Within the circle, imagine anyone who is sick or unhappy and ask that the healing power of the night may relieve them while they sleep.

- When you are ready, thank the guardians and bid them farewell, beginning in the North and walking around the circle clockwise.

- Then stand facing your altar looking North and thank your own special angel or guardian.

- Finally, uncast your circle by walking around it anti-clockwise, saying: 'May the circle that is cast remain unbroken in our hearts and in our minds as here it stood in this sacred place for my ceremony. Blessings be.'

- Stay quietly in the remaining candlelight and when you are ready extinguish the final candle, sending its light to anyone you know will be lying awake worrying or unhappy.

- Clear and tidy everything away and then enjoy a drink or light meal while listening to music.

Creating Night Rituals

The above ceremony can form a basic template for night rituals.

A variation is to bless and empower with each of the four elements in turn a symbol or photograph of what it is you wish to draw into your life or to heal. This may be a place, person or animal in need of strength. In the same way, you can empower a special crystal or small pot of flowers that you can then send to someone who is ill.

In the next chapter we will look at ways of banishing negativity and psychically cleansing and protecting ourselves while working night magic.

2

Psychic Protection at Night

Fears are magnified at night when the world is quiet and filled with shadows. Even successful adults may fear darkness, while children may sleep with the light on because they do not understand the powers of the night that their innate sensitivity amplifies.

The worst spectres of the night may be those we project from within ourselves once the rigid blocking mechanism of daytime consciousness has relaxed. This can be especially true if we are a kind, gentle person and absorb the problems or spite of others. Therefore clearing our own inner residue of suppressed negativity is the first step to night-time protection.

Banishing Personal Negativity

Casting away personal negativity at the end of the day and certainly before sleep is spiritually cleansing, especially at times of stress or unavoidable conflict in your daily life. We can carry money or family worries with us when we go to bed and these can keep us awake or be translated into anxiety dreams. Such fears are counterproductive, leaving us exhausted and defeated before we begin the next day. What is more, they can prevent us from finding a creative solution, which may come naturally in sleep.

Until the 18th century, corked stone or Bellarmine jars filled with brass and iron nails, rosemary and urine were used as charms against evil and evil-doers, especially in East Anglia and the Netherlands. The bottles would be buried beneath a doorstep to protect a home.

In the modern world we can adapt this practice, substituting soured red wine as the protective liquid, to neutralise unwanted mental clutter and then bury it. You can buy old stone jars with corks at car boot or garage sales or use new ones containing cider. However, you can use any dark jar with a screw-on lid, even a coffee jar.

Prepare a supply of pliant metal, either in the form of paper clips or small pieces of thin wire you can pre-cut with pliers. Iron was a traditionally protective metal. Also have ready a small pot of living rosemary or a dish of dried rosemary.

Method for Banishing Negativity

- When not in use, keep your negativity pot corked and covered with a dark cloth in a high place near the front door. You could erect a small Bellarmine shelf with lots of tiny pots of greenery to keep the atmosphere pure. Otherwise leave your negativity pot outside the front door where it will not be disturbed.

- The first time you use your jar, add a sprinkling of salt to cleanse it psychically, plus a handful of soil. Thereafter add salt each time before use to prevent any negativity coming from the jar as you add new metal.

- When darkness falls after a difficult day, sit with your dish of metal and uncork your jar. As you sprinkle the salt into the jar, say: 'Purity, sanctity, absorb negativity.'

- Take a paper clip or a small piece of wire and bend it so that the ends cross over. Continue to bend the wire until it occupies as small a space as possible.

- As you do so, name an anger or sorrow left over from the day and then place your metal knot in the jar, saying: 'Thus unwind, knot I bind, peace to find. Go in peace to be healed and restored by Mother Earth.'

- If there is more than one issue you wish to unburden, make as many wire knots as necessary.

- When you have finished, add a sprig of rosemary or some of the dried herb, saying, 'Rosemary for remembrance, only peace and happiness will I recall this night.'

- Cork the jar and replace it beneath the cover in its high place.

- When your jar is about two-thirds full, add a little sour red wine, cork the jar and shake it, saying: 'Ferment and sleep in the arms of the Mother, no more to harm or disturb my night-time tranquillity.'

- When it is very dark, bury the jar in the garden, in a deep flower bed outside an apartment, or dispose of it where it will be taken away as rubbish.

Psychic Cleansing

In the last chapter I talked about having a special bath or shower before beginning psychic work. You can also use baths with gently cleansing oils such as rose or chamomile or essential oil shower gels to wash away general negativity.

Other methods include running your fingers through your aura or psychic energy field above your head, as you would brush your hair, using gentle circular movements with both hands, first anti-clockwise and then clockwise. You may feel tangles coming out.

Before you begin, hold your arms straight above your head. That is the general aura width and the aura then follows down the body in a sphere shape. With your arms outstretched you may feel a slight rubbery sensation as you hit the outer part of the aura. You can cleanse the whole aura by working from the top of the head to the shoulders. You can also bathe yourself in purple light from a candle by breathing in the light (*see pages 17–19*).

Another method of clearing emotional clutter is to smudge around yourself with some sage incense or a smudge stick by wafting it all around you from toe to head and down again in anti-clockwise circles, then up again in clockwise circles.

Protection Against the Malevolence of Others

Most of what we absorb and banish in the stone jar is material we have unconsciously absorbed. However, there are times when we are subject to more intensive psychological attack, perhaps from a spiteful colleague, an abusive relation or a jealous neighbour. A rival in love or career may even deliberately wish us ill. This attack may not be confined to daytime contact and the darkness can make it seem even more intense. The person may gossip or complain about us during the evening or think angry thoughts as they lie in bed fretting.

Psychic attack rarely involves someone sticking pins in an image or burning a black candle while reciting our name backwards. However, bad thoughts winging towards us in the darkness when we are especially receptive can be very invasive.

Of course any negativity does rebound threefold on the sender, but it is important to shield yourself, your loved ones and your home from unwelcome thought power. You may wish to cast routine protection around your home and loved ones, just as you would habitually lock the door at night.

Psychic Protection at Night for Your Home

People living in areas of high crime and vandalism may especially find that protective rituals when it gets dark or before bed help in creating ongoing vibrations that make strangers less likely to attack or cause trouble near the home. There are several ways of protecting your home.

Dark Crystal Sentinels

Crystals of the night and the Moon are an instant but potent guard against hostility. Use amethyst, angelite/celestite, Apache tears/obsidian, smoky quartz, purple and green fluorite, rutilated quartz, jet, blue beryl, rose quartz, moonstone/selenite, garnet, jade, mother of pearl, opal, onyx, sodalite or dark agates. Amethysts are soothing in bedrooms and rose quartz and jade are wonderful for children. This is because they release their gentle energies slowly and so do not overwhelm little ones. Dark agates are powerful in entrances or street windows.

'Setting' Crystals for Protection

• Create a small set of protective crystals and leave them when not in use in a covered bowl with a large chunk of unpolished amethyst as a cleanser. Rest the amethyst in the earth occasionally to restore its energies.

• You can charge your crystals with protective power by setting the dish in full moonlight once a month or by sprinkling them with Moon water (*see pages 55–6*).

• As it becomes dark, move the palms of your hands downwards in circles nine times, the left clockwise, the right anti-clockwise, a few inches over the dish of crystals, saying, 'Guardian of the crystals [or the name of your favourite Dark Archangel], may none enter – person, thought or harmful energy – while you stand watch over my home and all I love.'

• Beginning with the rooms at the top of your house and working downwards from front to back, set a dark crystal on each window ledge inside the room, so it can catch any moonlight.

• Next, place small pieces of unpolished amethyst on either side of the front and back doors, the most pointed end outwards for defence. 'Point outwards' is a good general rule when using crystals for protection.

• Finally, as close to the centre of the house downstairs or in the middle of the apartment as you can, put a small dark round crystal sphere on a low table.

• Hold this central crystal between your hands and breathe on to it three times, with each breath seeing the protective light spiralling outwards.

• Collect your crystals about once a week in the morning and run each under water for cleansing before returning them to the bowl. You can cover it in a dark cloth until nightfall. If you or your family are under psychic attack, cleanse them more often and pass the smoke of cleansing incense such as pine or eucalyptus over the bowl of crystals before use in the evening.

Crystals are an easy but effective way of protecting your home and it takes only a minute to set your sentinel crystals at the same time as you lock the doors.

Children especially can appreciate a crystal guardian in their bedroom at night. Also set crystals permanently in any dark areas where you keep your possessions, such as garages, sheds and outhouses. Sometimes people can focus unconscious malevolence as envy of one of our possessions. This was called 'putting on the evil eye' in earlier times.

You can also bury large rough-cut dark crystals at the boundaries of your land or in a plant pot outside your front door.

Making a Crystal Amulet

A crystal can make a good protective amulet if you or a family member has to travel at night or if you feel vulnerable in a dark place. Night crystal amulets will also help a child or adult facing bullying during the day.

- To empower the crystal, wait until dusk is falling. Work in the open air or near an open window to absorb the power of the night. A windy night when the air is circulating is especially good.

- Sprinkle the crystal with salt, circle a night incense around it, pass it across the flame of a dark red or silver candle and finally sprinkle it with Moon water or pure spring water. As you do so, recite: 'Earth, Air, Fire and Water, as the Sun sets, power of dark, Air, Earth, Water, Fire, kindle this protective spark.'

- Make the chant faster until on the final 'spark' you hold the crystal over the candle once more. Blow out the candle, projecting its light into the crystal.

Keep your crystal amulet in a tiny pouch or purse. If you are alone or afraid, hold it and see the light pouring from it and encircling you.

You might also like to attach a tiny protective crystal to your pet's collar if it is a night roamer, such as a cat, or is in a vulnerable place, such as a field or stable. Place a crystal amulet in a rabbit or guinea-pig hutch and or a bird cage.

Earth Guardians

If you have ever visited an ancient stone circle as night falls you may be aware of huge brown shadowy figures almost like dark tongues of flame. You may catch a glimpse of them too as you walk along an ancient traders' track on a dark winter's afternoon.

In traditional belief in Western Europe and Scandinavia each area has its special land wights or earth spirits who traditionally guard settlements, standing watch from dusk until the morning. You met a similar concept in the guardians of the four main directions. You can tune in to the energies of the watchers of your own piece of land, even if you share it with other apartments.

In traditional manner, too, you should leave offerings for the watchers – dark crystals, flowers, berries and silver coins in tiny pots hidden close to your boundaries. Add an offering every few days or whenever you feel in need of extra protection. You can bury the contents of the pot when it is full and give any money to charity.

If you do feel under threat psychically or psychologically or your home is in an area that has problems with crime, light four candles to invoke the earth sentinels at the four main directions in the room nearest to the centre of your home. You can do this in addition to or as a substitute for the protective crystals.

Calling the Earth Guardians in the Candle

- Choose a room that represents the heart of your home, a place where you spend a lot of time. Alternatively, take a photograph of your family members, not forgetting pets, standing outside the home, and set it on your night altar.

- For this ritual use rich brown candles in all four directions, set against the four walls of the room.

- Wait until dusk, then light each candle, beginning in the North, while visualising a pillar of brown light forming into the guardian of each of the four directions. As you invoke them more frequently you may notice subtle differences in their nature.

- Beginning in the North, say: 'Bless and protect my home this night, Wise Watcher of the North,' then add any specific areas of threat or uncertainty, worries you have about psychic attack, children's fears of the dark, care of particular animals, etc.

- Repeat the invocation as you light the candles of the East, South and West in turn.

- Leave the candles burning for a while and then blow them out in reverse order of lighting, projecting the light to the watchers at the actual boundaries of your home.

- If you pass a window and look into the darkness you may see a tall flickering shadow and know you are safe from all harm.

Using Candles

The act of lighting night candles in your home is in itself a way of drawing protection to the home and its inhabitants. You can fragrance your candles with night scents if you wish for additional blessings on yourself and your home.

Use dark red, silver, dark green, deep purple, midnight blue and burnished gold candles.

Using Night Incenses and Oils

Burning incense and oils of the night in your home is another potent way of creating protection. As well as clearing malevolence from earthly forces, throughout the ages incense has been a cleanser of the paranormal negativity that may come either from unfriendly ghosts or from negative psychic earth energies (*see page 36*).

I have already described smudging or smoke power (*see page 29*). The general rule is to light your smudge or incense stick and move it (and yourself for a large space) rhythmically over what is to be cleansed. Use anti-clockwise circles for removing darkness and clockwise for adding light. Let your body take over and flow with the smoke.

Unfriendly Ghosts

You can tell if you have any negative phantoms even if you have not seen a ghost. Animals will growl in certain rooms and children may complain of a dark figure that scowls at them or tells them to go away. You may feel you are being watched or items go missing, only to reappear in the place you left them hours or days later.

Your negative presence will be felt or seen most clearly at night. In most cases the ghost is not bad but unhappy. They may not be deliberately spooking you but may have been hurt by people during life or may feel that you are invading their home.

Note down places where the presence has been most clearly experienced and walk around with your arms outstretched, palms facing outwards, barefoot, using the energy centres in your feet and hands to detect what may feel like jarring mild electric shocks, unpleasant shivers or even a thin invisible membrane in the outline of a body. (Friendly presences are light as gossamer and feel welcoming.)

You may find your ghost has created a path where they regularly pace up and down. There is often one spot where the ghost usually appears and three or four less frequented areas. Plot these and the 'ghost path', if there is one, on a plan of your home.

Clearing a Ghost Path

- Each night in the room where the ghost is felt most strongly, light a soft dusky pink or purple candle and burn a gentle incense such as rose.

- Sit quietly and talk to the ghost, explaining that you are sorry they are unhappy and suggesting they might wish to move on to where friends or family may be waiting.

- Whisper: 'Go in peace, friend, or if you wish to stay, remain as a welcome guest also in peace.'

- Blow out the candle and open the window, visualising a pathway of light rising up into the sky along which the ghost can travel.

- Continue making the sky path lighter each night until you can visualise a sphere of light at the end. You may feel the atmosphere in your home lightening as the ghost departs or lets go of their bitterness. If not, try the method I suggest below for cleansing your home of negative earth power. This will help the ghost to let go of the Earth.

Negative Earth Energies

Even if you have identified a ghost, test for negative earth energies, the other cause of psychic unrest in a home. Often the two are linked and the ghost is using the negative power to fuel their hostility, just as friendly phantoms derive power from positive earth energies.

Negative earth energies can be caused by psychic power that is too intense or concentrated for a dwelling. They can also develop if a ley or subterranean psychic energy channel has become blocked or soured, either by earthly pollution or by unhappy or bad deeds that occurred on the site hundreds or even thousands of years earlier.

Negative earth energies tend to be manifest as regular grid squares two or three feet in area. They are also experienced as continuous lines anything from a few inches to several feet wide extending across a particular room from the front to the back or in a main corridor. This passageway or any rooms the negative energies cross may always seem dark and cold. Plants will not thrive there and animals will not sleep, especially where the flow is blocked. You may find that you feel tired and out of sorts, or that inexplicable quarrels break out regularly over these concentrated psychic stagnation pools.

Locating Negative Earth Energies

- Wait until after dark, when you will find it easier to sense the negative earth energies.

- First note if there are any particular spots where you consistently and without reason feel irritable or where your partner seems to stand when they yell at you. Do the children or the cats always fight in the hallway?

- Mark these places on a plan of your home.

- Carrying your pendulum, walk across the rooms and corridors where you detect this negative feeling. You will find that at intervals the pendulum spirals anti-clockwise, as if caught in a vortex, but at the same time feels incredibly heavy. This will be quite unlike the sensation of encountering a friendly ghost. These points will coincide with those locations where it seems always dark and unfriendly. In some cases you may find that the most concentrated unfriendly ghost spots also coincide with the blocked earth energies.

If your resident ghost is still causing trouble, the following should help them to move on as well as remove the negative earth powers.

Cleansing Negative Energies Using Night Incenses

- Choose powerful cleansing incense – patchouli and pine are especially good. Use two broad-based incense sticks that you can carry safely around the house. Cross them and move your hands in circles, holding the sticks almost upright so the smoke mingles.

- First cleanse each room, whether or not it is a ghost spot or a negative earth stream course. Begin upstairs on the left as you enter the house.

- In each room or passage start in the left-hand corner nearest the door, moving your left hand clockwise and right anti-clockwise in unison.

- Move in a clockwise direction around each room, circling your sticks as you walk.

- Do the same for corridors, still travelling from upstairs to downstairs, front to back, until you have visited every part of your home. Remember to include attics and cellars.

- Next focus on the lines of negative energy/ghost paths, again beginning at the top left of the house and moving left to right or front to back. Keep circling the incense as you walk.

- Finally, stand in each of the negative spots and turn around three times clockwise with your smoke sticks, saying: 'Friend or stagnant pool of power, move on and away in the name of peace, goodness and light, if it is right to be.' You may be rewarded by a momentary flash of light and a sense of peace.

- Repeat this weekly until the effect is gone.

- Place tiny amethysts close to the main circles of negativity to keep them pure.

- Finally, place amethyst or crystals where the energy starts from, usually against a wall or near an entrance. You can generally sense the swirl, like a blocked drain, but if not, walk around the inner walls with your pendulum and you will experience an incredibly powerful anti-clockwise spiralling and perhaps a feeling of nausea.

If the phantom still does not leave or become more benign, you might consider asking a sympathetic priest, a reputable medium or a spiritual healer to carry out a blessing ceremony in your home.

Using Healing Light

If you are in the depths of darkest despair, you can use this simple method to help you through the night. It also overcomes fear of physical darkness. Most of all, it is a very powerful method of self-healing, whether for the body, heart or soul. The night seems to amplify healing, as the body is at rest and the mind open to spiritual powers.

The Blessing of Healing Light

Practise this first by candlelight, using a pure white or beeswax candle, or use a white fibre-optic light that casts shimmering beams in the air. A lava lamp with golden bubbles can also be effective.

- Light the candle or lamp and allow yourself to absorb the light through every pore.

- Raise your hands and extend your fingertips towards the source of light, drawing it in through your fingertips by breathing gently but deeply and imagining a magnet within each finger. You may feel liquid light running up your arms and flowing downwards into your heart where the chakra or energy centre that controls the hand chakra points resides. You may feel warm, relaxed and at peace, perhaps for the first time in ages, and feel terror, tension or actual pain fading.

- Now the light is within and you can extinguish the external source of light.

- As you relax you can see your body slightly luminous in the darkness and sense your aura sparkling with beams and tiny rays of light.

- Next you need to create a circuit for the light. If you are afraid or anxious rather than physically or emotionally ill or in pain, place your hands in the centre of your stomach.

- Move your hand up slightly towards your chest until your feel a whirling centre of energy. This is your solar plexus or Sun chakra, the psychic energy centre that gives us the ability to determine our own fate and to resist attack, whether from internal fears or external forces, earthly or paranormal.

- When you have found this psychic centre, press gently with your left hand beneath your right so that the light flows from your fingertips into the chakra, which may become quite hot.

- The room may seem momentarily bright and after a minute or so you will experience the two-way flow as the light travels back and forth as the circuit is made.

- When you feel calm and happy, gently remove your hands. This may feel like pulling off an adhesive.

- Sit and enjoy the gentle humming, buzzing sensation within your whole body and mind.

- If you have a particularly painful area of your body or are ill and know the seat of your illness, apply your hands to that place and use that as the entry point.

- If you are generally ill or exhausted, you can apply the light to the centre of your hairline.

Night healing can be sent to other people, animals or places. Hold your light-charged fingers over a photograph or symbol of who or what needs healing. You can also direct the light towards family members who are away from home at night, out in the darkness or in a potentially dangerous night place.

The greatest protection is always working with good intent and holding within yourself a core of light and calmness. This is not easy, but as you work more with night energies and your inner stillness increases, so your need for external forms of protection will diminish.

In the next chapter we will work with the energies of the Moon, which for millennia has formed the focus of night ritual and has been the traditional marker of the natural cycles of human life.

3

Moon Power

The night has her own special light that has had magical significance in all cultures. Wherever we see the Moon, whether over the rooftops, rising from the sea or illuminating woodlands, her light will transform the scene into a place of enchantment, mystery and beauty.

Each month the Moon is born out of the darkness, grows, becomes full, then decreases until she disappears into the darkness once more. Three days later she is reborn. This birth/maturity, death/rebirth cycle gave rise to the belief that the Moon was mother of plants, humans and animals.

The energies of the Moon, which are regarded traditionally as female, have many functions in our daily as well as magical life. Just as the Moon energises the tides, so she also affects our emotions and bodily fluids. In women she influences menstruation and fertility. But in men too she can cause mood swings, especially around the full Moon.

By tuning into the Moon's ebbs and flows we can become more harmonious. We can use the waxing and waning energies to bring to the fore different aspects of ourselves, so that we are more outgoing on the increasing tide and rest and reflect more on the ebb.

The Moon Goddess

One of the most important symbols in night magic is the goddess of the Moon, whether she represents to you an aspect of the Great Goddess or is regarded as a symbol of the mystery and spirituality of lunar energies.

The Moon goddess has been worshipped in many forms through the ages. We know that the ancient Egyptians invoked Isis, the Moon mother, her consort Osiris and their son Horus, the sky god, the original Holy Trinity, in their crescent Moon wishes, but we are not sure when the custom began.

Tuscan witches, whose cult to Diana, the Classical Moon goddess, may have started before 500 BC, believe that by dividing herself, Diana created all things. In popular myths in a number of lands it is told that the Moon took dead souls back to her womb to await fertilisation by the Sun and rebirth.

The Triple Goddess of the Three Phases

The Triple Goddess – maiden, mother and crone, reflecting the three main lunar phases of waxing, full and waning – is found in many cultures from India to ancient Greece. One of her earliest representations is a trinity of huge carved stone goddesses found in a cave at the Abri du Roc aux Sorciers at Angles-sur-l'Anglin in France and dating from between 13,000 and 11,000 BC.

Though the Moon has eight astronomical phases, it is the three phases corresponding to maiden, mother and crone that are the most significant in psychic work and in ritual. By tuning in to the physical Moon we can understand and harness these distinct energy phases in our daily as well as magical world.

In the maiden phase, for example, I try to set everything in motion for the month, from planning my work to my finances and putting in extra writing time while I am energetic. I send out proposals for new projects and try to get the children from under their duvets and on to their life paths – or at least to tidy their rooms.

Around the full Moon I am either wildly optimistic that I will be the next J. K. Rowling or planning my escape from the creditors to Spain to read the Tarot in a beach hut. This is the time I am most inspired and also most likely to throw the china.

By the wane, it is clearing the unpaid bills and unfinished business of the month, binning a few unfulfilled dreams and trying to get a few hours to myself so I am not too ratty. As the waning Moon phase develops, I try to encourage the children away from dangerous pursuits, from giving up on school or life (though I sympathise) or from locking horns with their father over who rules the forest.

Some people work with Diana, the Classical Moon goddess, in all the phases. However, one of the most popular trinities is made up of the Greek Artemis as the waxing Moon maiden, Selene as the Moon mother and Hecate, crone goddess of the waning and dark Moon.

You might like to find images of these goddesses in books or art galleries (or even download them from the Internet), so that when you work with the actual Moon in the sky you can visualise the goddesses (though of course you can picture the forms in any way you wish or substitute a triple Moon god – son, father and grand-father). I will describe some of the qualities of each and you can then create rituals that draw on the different energy phases.

Artemis

Artemis is the goddess of the hunt as well as the Moon and has been known under different names from Neolithic times. She was described as the twin sister of the young Graeco-Roman Sun god Apollo and travelled the night sky in a silver chariot pulled by white stags, shooting silver shafts of moonlight and subjecting even the great sea god Poseidon to her sway as she controlled the tides.

At the new Moon she was worshipped in the form of the Great She Bear by her virgin priestesses and she is also an aspect of the virgin White Goddess immortalised by the poet and historian Robert Graves, who, he believed, inspired men to poetry and women to magic.

Artemis is the challenger who drives us ever onwards, especially at the waxing time, to explore, to challenge old ideas within ourselves and not to compromise our integrity for approval.

Selene

The phase of the full Moon is attributed to Selene, or Luna to the Romans. Twin sister of Helios, the older Greek Sun god, she rose from the sea in her chariot drawn by white horses at night and rode high in the sky at full Moon.

Selene was a prolific mother, producing Pandia, goddess of brightness, Ersa, goddess of the dew, and Nemea, the mountain goddess. By the mortal Endymion she had 50 daughters, each, it is said, symbolising one of the lunar months (of 29.5 days) between the ancient Olympic Games.

A goddess of marriage, married women and mothers, Selene is also mistress of enchantment and magical ritual. Not surprisingly at the full Moon she is invoked for fertility by women eager to conceive, and is goddess of mothers and all who seek the power of intuition and inspiration.

Hecate

The phase of the waning and dark of the Moon belongs to Hecate, goddess of the side of the Moon that is not visible from Earth. Hecate is the goddess of the Underworld as well as the Moon and serves as a guide through the darkness with her torch.

Hecate is also goddess of the crossroads, where offerings were left for her at midnight, especially at triple crossroads, the intersection of past, present and future. In the British Museum in London there is a triple Hecate statuette of three women facing three directions with linked hands. Hecate was regarded as the goddess of rebirth, secrets and dreams, and of sailors, because of her role as controller of the tides. She was also Mistress of Enchantment.

Hecate is the wise friend who will never tell you life is easy and the film always ends happily, but will hold your hand if the night seems too long and lonely.

Isis, Moon Goddess of Enchantment

However, for thousands of years, the most significant goddess for lunar magic has been the ancient Egyptian Isis. Goddess of the Moon and sea, she was often depicted wearing a crown that represented the full Moon, held within the crescents of the waxing and waning Moons.

Though she was one of the great goddesses of Egypt, worship of Isis became equally popular in the Greek and Roman worlds, particularly among women. Her cult spread throughout Europe as far north as England, but Paris was Isis's special city. One school of thought says the name is a corruption of Par-Isis, By Isis.

Isis was named Lady of Lunar Enchantment in the novels of the

20th-century occultist Dion Fortune. In the modern world, she remains a central figure in goddess-focused organisations such as the Fellowship of Isis, which has members worldwide.

The second-century writer Apuleius, who was born in the Roman colony of Madura in Morocco and was initiated into the Mysteries of Isis, described her as an ethereal goddess of magic in his semi-autobiographical work *The Golden Ass*:

> *From the sea began to rise the apparition of a woman. So lovely was her face that the gods themselves would have knelt in adoration. Crowning her long, thick hair was an intricate chaplet, in which was woven every kind of flower. Just above her brow shone a disc like a mirror, bright as the face of the Moon, and this told me who she was. Glittering stars were embroidered round the hem of her mantle and adorning her was a full and fiery Moon.*

This image of Isis is one that has formed the basis for recent art, literature and her role as Lady of the Magical Arts in the late 19th- and early 20th-century Western magical tradition, notably the Golden Dawn occult society.

In her novel *The Sea Priestess*, Dion Fortune gave a similar description. In accordance with the Western magical tradition, she distinguishes between Isis Veiled, the heavenly Isis, Lady of the Moon, and Isis Unveiled, the goddess of nature, mother of the Sun.

Isis will connect you with magic and with the deep mysteries of womanhood and the joys and pains of caring for others, being loyal and overcoming any difficulties with serenity and dignity.

The Moon Goddess and the Sea

The goddess of the Moon is closely linked to the tidal waters of the Earth and so is also often honoured as the goddess of the sea.

Like Isis, the Virgin Mary was associated with the Moon, with a crescent Moon at her feet, and, as Stella Maris, star of the sea, in a star-spangled robe. You can offer prayers to her in any lunar ritual.

The Moon goddess is also depicted in the form of a mermaid, for example Yemanja (also called Yamaya) of Nigeria and Brazil. Yemanja is portrayed walking upon the waves of the ocean and adorned with the crescent Moon. She is called the Womb of Creation and is the bringer of dreams and prosperity. In Brazil, on New Year's Eve, her worshippers create altars on the shore with candles and food that are accepted by Yemanja on the morning tide.

A Full Moon and Sea Ritual

In the Western magical tradition, too, fires are created at night below high-water mark, to be surrounded by and eventually consumed by the sea. This ritual combines the four ancient elements of Water, Air, Earth and Fire, while recognising the superiority of the primal waters.

Performed on the night of the full Moon, the most powerful astrological day of change each month, this can be a very powerful way of giving impetus to a important, long-term aim, whether for an internal or external change. It is also an excellent way of getting in touch with lunar energies if you find it hard to connect on a deep spiritual level and so can be very helpful for men as well as women.

You may have to wait and study tide tables and lunar cycles to get the conditions just right.

You can work inland and improvise in lots of ways, making your fire on the night of the full Moon just before a predicted rainfall or working on a non-tidal river, pool or lake. Then you would put out your fire with water at the time of high tide at your nearest coastal water, even if it is hundreds of miles away. However, if possible, you should attempt a full sea or tidal river and Moon ritual at least once. This will help you to visualise the power when you carry your symbolic inland rituals.

You can also work in the later stages of the waxing Moon or, if you want to banish something, on the wane. You can use the full Moon for attracting or banishing rites.

• When the full or near full Moon is shining on the shore, create a fire just below the high-tide line as the tide is coming in (be careful to check times and make sure you don't get cut off). You can identify this high point by the line of beach debris that may still be damp. You may need to use a firm wood base or even stones for the fire.

• As you build your fire, which need only be small, endow each piece of driftwood with a wish or empowerment and visualise the fruition of your purpose as you work.

- Prepare small offerings to cast on to the fire as gifts to the Moon/sea goddess, whom you may name or visualise as the magical rays of energy radiating from the glowing orb in the sky. You could use dried herbs, flowers or, for what you want to lose, dead leaves or twigs. Burning offerings can either send particular energies to be amplified by the cosmos or cast out what you wish to lose from your life. The words and symbols you use will define the purpose.

- Just before high tide, light the fire and as you cast each flower or handful of herbs on to it, make an empowerment prayer or wish aloud, asking the Moon goddess to endow her power and blessing to your endeavour.

- When you have finished, retreat above the tide line and watch as the tide carries the fire to the Moon and the elements come together.

Working with the Moon Goddess

Because human bodies contain a high proportion of water, some say that the Moon also influences our hormonal and emotional ebbs and flows. She can attune men as well as women to their true feelings, especially the inner radar that taps information not available to the conscious mind.

This connection with our subtle psychic powers can be made and strengthened by working with the Moon. Once you have awoken this ability, it can be used in your everyday life, by day as well as night, not least because at certain times of the month the Moon is in the sky during daylight.

Unlike the Sun, which clearly marks the horizons of what can be achieved, the Moon says that anything is possible while she holds sway. The problems of daily life can be resolved creatively and with inspiration once the barriers of harsh light have fallen and we attune to the ocean of limitless space and time.

Living by the Moon

Hunter-gatherers and later farmers recorded the lunar cycle as marks on rock, bone or wood, creating the earliest calendars. In contemporary indigenous traditions such as the Native American, the names of the different full Moons still echo the qualities of each season. Since these show a remarkable similarity to the Celtic calendar 2,000 years earlier, it may be that the full Moons were markers for different activities, such as the coming of the herds or birds. For example, the April/May Moon in the Celtic world was called Glamonios, which means Growing Green Shoots. In the Native American tradition it was called Frog or Blossom Moon, reflecting the mating of the frogs after their winter hibernation.

Over the next year you can create names for each of the Moons to reflect the events in your world, whether urban or rural. For example, to the Celts, the January Moon was Angantios, Staying at Home Moon, and to the Native Americans Gnawing on Bones Moon. For me, the full Moon in January is Reckoning Moon, when my very chaotic tax accounts are due. Also after Christmas it really is a time for assessing what works and does not work financially, career-wise and emotionally.

My September full Moon I call Fading Summer Moon. The site by the sea where I have my caravan closes the following month and I am sad because I will soon be losing my sanctuary for the four months of winter. The nights are drawing in fast and so I squeeze in every possible moment outdoors, sitting by candlelight outside the caravan and watching the stars, ignoring the growing chill and the advancing mud.

Whenever possible in September I feed the wild geese at the local bird conservation park. The geese are filled with the same awareness that summer is almost gone and they are already practising flying in formation and becoming less interested in the visitors. This is quite in tune with the Celtic Song Moon and the Native American When the Geese Fly South Moon.

Your Moon Calendar

You can set up your own Moon calendar by following these simple steps.

- Divide the year into 13 approximately four-week periods. Moon months vary slightly in length. Use a diary marking full Moons to make your calendar and start with day 1 and lunar month 1 as the nearest full Moon to when you begin. Of course, it does not matter how many full Moons are in the calendar year because once you have named your 13 full Moons you start again.

• Keep notes of how each full Moon makes you feel. Over a period of two or three lunar years you will discover definite energy patterns emerging so that you can plan your year to take advantage of the energies of the seasons.

Whether or not you create an ongoing personal Moon calendar, you can adapt the following ritual to focus on the different energies emanated by the full Moon in the different seasons.

Your Moon Calendar Full Moon Ritual

• On the day of the full Moon, create your provisional title for the Moon, taking into account the weather around that period, any major seasonal events such as Christmas and the personal significance of the month for you. You may find that you change the names over the years.

• Choose a symbol or picture to represent the energies of the month. I would use a pottery goose or a picture of migrating geese for my September Moon, for example.

• On the evening of the full Moon, or as close as you can, light a circle of small silver-coloured candles around the symbol. Place this in the centre of your night altar on a circle of silver foil. Silver is the colour and metal of the Moon. If you cannot find silver candles, white ones will be fine.

• Light one of the Moon incenses (*see page 52*), for example jasmine or mimosa, and make yourself a tiny wooden wand from a willow branch or any other tree or plant that grows near water.

• Take a silver coin and place it on top of or next to the symbol on the foil circle.

• Pass your wand through the smoke of the incense and the flame of the candle so that it singes but does not ignite. As you do so, say: 'Air of the night air, light in the darkness, Mother Moon, I charge this tree wand with your radiance.'

• Circle the symbol and coin with nine clockwise casts of the Moon wand, listing nine strengths you seek in the coming month. Name your Moon nine times and end by saying: 'Bring opportunity, joy and prosperity. Thus, Moon Mother, I do greet thee.'

• Blow out the candles one at a time, repeating the strengths you seek, and leave the incense burning.

• Go out into the garden or open a window and if the Moon is shining, face her or face the direction where you see the glimmer of brightness behind the clouds.

• Raise your wand to the sky, point it down to the earth and to the four directions, beginning in the North, and repeating: 'Bring opportunity, joy and prosperity. Thus, Moon Mother, I do greet thee.'

• Repeat your nine empowerments as you gaze up at the Moon.

• When you are ready, go indoors and set your symbol and coin on the silver foil on the window ledge until the next morning. Then place them on your night altar until the next full Moon.

Working with the Moon

In magic, as in astrology, the Moon is regarded as a planet. In fact, she is a satellite, the closest heavenly body to Earth and the brightest after the Sun.

The Moon's light increases from right to left until the full Moon and thereafter decreases also from right to left until the final crescent on the left disappears. About two and a half days later the crescent appears again on the right.

If you want to be a real purist, remember that the Moon is full at the second it rises and thereafter wanes. But in practice, full Moon energies are from Moon rise to set and the hours immediately around that period.

The best way to understand the Moon is to watch her in the sky over the course of several months, creating markers of buildings, chimneys, trees or hills or even when she shines in your bedroom window. You will discover a pattern in her movements. Chart the way the different phases make you feel.

Though there are slight variations each month, the order of the Moon's phases and basic energies remains the same all year. Most newspapers will tell you when the Moon rises and sets and the phase, or you can find out from a Moon diary or online almanac. It is worth planning your Moon magic a month or so ahead to take advantage of the increase or decrease of lunar energies.

Attuning to the Moon's Phases

Just as the different monthly energies will reflect and amplify your feelings, so within the month your emotions will also vary. Of course, this will not depend entirely on the Moon, but if you focus on the Moon you may discover that certain moods or desires emerge. Do you want to clear a cupboard, dance or curl up with a book? Over the months you will detect patterns in the different phases that may explain seemingly irrational moods.

Women are especially strongly affected by lunar energies. Indeed, before the advent of electric light, women would menstruate at the dark of the Moon or very close to it and so premenstrual tension would occur during the waning Moon when the natural energies were advocating slowing down and resting.

Women who work regularly with lunar energies find that gradually their menstrual cycle does move so that peak fertility occurs at the full Moon (hence the association with love in earlier societies).

Moon Magic in Your Life

Go outdoors and focus on the Moon or where it should be. In the later part of the waning phase the Moon does not rise till very late in the evening, so you may prefer to work before dawn the next day, when you can see it shining like a jewel in the early morning sky. You can visualise the Moon if it is cloudy.

Though I have suggested rituals for the three main phases, you can devise your own to harness the prevailing mood of the Moon.

Substances of the Moon

Here is a list of various Moon substances you may find useful in your work. These all seem to work well with lunar energies and have traditionally been used in a number of cultures.

Incense and oils Clary sage, chamomile, freesia, gardenia, jasmine, lemon balm, lily, lotus, mimosa, myrrh, poppy, rosewood, wintergreen and ylang ylang. (Some oils are not suitable for personal use or inhalation in pregnancy, for example clary sage, myrrh, poppy and wintergreen, so check labels and if in doubt ask a pharmacist.)

Trees Alder, coconut, eucalyptus, lemon tree, silver birch, sycamore, tamarind, willow, all trees that grow by water

Element Water

Colour Silver or white

Crystals Moonstone, angelite/celestite, mother of pearl, pearl, selenite, opal

Metal Silver

Day of the week Monday is the day associated with lunar goddesses and with the planet in traditional magic. Monday is named after the Moon.

Archangel Gabriel (*see page 120*)

The Waxing Moon

Use the waxing Moon for new beginnings and longer-term goals; improving health; the gradual increase of prosperity; attracting good luck; fertility magic; finding friendship, new love and romance; job hunting; making plans for the future and increasing psychic awareness.

In many cultures people turn over silver coins or jewellery three times when the crescent Moon appears in the sky and make a wish. As the Moon grows, it is believed that prosperity and good luck will grow too.

Begin waxing Moon magic when you can see the crescent in the sky and continue until the day before the full Moon. You can repeat a wish or empowerment nightly if necessary each waxing Moon period for projects that will take months or even a year or more to bring to fruition.

The closer to the full Moon, the more intense the energies. A personally devised ritual using your Moon substances over three days up to and including the full Moon is excellent for an urgent project or one with a necessarily short time-scale.

The following ritual is a gentle way of filling yourself with optimism and the energy to make the coming month really significant in a positive way.

Breathing in the Moonlight

- Work outdoors and face the Moon.

- Place your focal crystal or large Moon crystals on a low stone or table in front of you.

- Sit on grass, earth or sand, on a blanket if it is cold.

- Begin by earthing yourself so that the power can flow through you but maintain connection with the land so that you do not become overwhelmed. Unearthed Moon power can feel like standing in a fast-flowing stream. The closer to the full Moon you work, the more powerful the flow. If possible, stand in a pool of moonlight.

- Press downwards through your perineum, palms and soles of your feet and feel your own roots embedded in the ground.

- Now extend your arms upwards in an arc above your head, palms uppermost.

- Breathe in slowly and deeply, visualising the light entering through the crown of your head and your fingertips, turning your head and hands silver.

- Exhale and inhale slowly in a continuous cycle so that the silver spreads through you, filling you with a gentle but powerful light.

- As you look at the Moon, walk in your imagination on the surface, through the craters, weaving magical moonscapes, castles of light, mountains of crystal, the essence of the Moon rather than the actual form. (Over the months, you may sense that your imagination has been replaced by a stronger sensation of actual mind or astral body travel. You are rooted to the ground and so need not be afraid.)

- When you are filled with light, shake your fingers while remaining rooted in the earth and see silver rays emanating from you that you can direct to any place and for any purpose of increase.

- Say: 'I send light through the darkness to . . .' Name your focus and purpose and visualise your subject surrounded by a sphere of moonlight, healed, protected or empowered. You may like to use your crystal wand or silver knife in your power hand to direct the energies.

- Now take your focal crystal and hold it between your hands towards the Moon so that the light is reflected in it.

- Breathe the moonlight once more, but this time exhale your Moon breath on to the surface of the crystal, transferring your gaze between Moon and crystal in a steady rhythm. You may become aware that the crystal is gleaming, but if not, visualise the increased brightness and in time your clairvoyant eye will take over.

- When you sense your crystal is fully charged, carry it indoors and set it on the altar or if you are away from home wrap it in pure white silk until you can return it to the altar. Your crystal will fill you with positive intent, even during the waning cycle, for those times when you need optimism and confidence.

- Sit quietly in the moonlight making plans for the coming months.

- When you go indoors, light a silver candle to shine on the crystal.

The Full Moon

Use the full Moon for any immediate need; a sudden boost of power or courage; a change of career, location or travel; psychic protection; healing acute medical conditions; a large sum of money needed urgently; consummation of love or making a permanent love commitment; fidelity spells, especially if a relationship is looking shaky; justice, ambition and promotion.

This is the day of full power but also of instability, as astrologically the Moon is in opposition or in the opposite side of the sky to the Sun. Since the full Moon rises close to sunset you can have the Moon rising in the East and the Sun setting in the West, a powerful backdrop for any change you intend or wish to make. I once stood on a bridge on marshland on the Isle of Wight and experienced the crossover of energies. It is a bit like revving a car with the handbrake on and suddenly releasing the brake, a terrific leap forward mentally or spiritually.

Drawing Down the Moon

This rite is said to date back to the Dianic witches of Thessaly in ancient Greece and is still practised by some covens. However, channelling wisdom, either from the Moon or from your deep well of wisdom bounced off and amplified by the full Moon, can provide a rich source of inspiration for any and every aspect of your life. It can suddenly make matters clear, offer a totally unexpected solution to a problem or increase your psychic awareness and clairvoyant abilities.

Work outdoors in a circle of full moonlight if possible. A moonlit beach or any place near water is especially magical.

Even if the full Moon is hidden by thick cloud, the power is still there. You could, if necessary, create a circle of silver candles indoors to represent the hidden Moon and give you a focal point. You could even use a silver fibre-optic lamp to shed symbolic moonbeams. In such circumstances, you will either have to visualise the Moon above or place a glow in the dark sphere on the ceiling that will be illuminated by the candles.

I will describe the ideal setting.

- In the centre of the pool of moonlight on the ground, place a silver bowl filled with water and a hand mirror. Have a small dish of moonstones at the side.

- Begin by Moon breathing until you feel you are filled with light, then ground yourself with your feet. Tonight, however, we are going to allow the fast-flowing stream of Moon energy to carry us a little way.

- The simplest method of drawing down the Moon is to swirl yourself around until you become dizzy, then steady yourself and the physical Moon will rush towards you. Often you can use methods such as this to trick the conscious mind into allowing psychic impressions to pass through into the wise unconscious. You are also creating a channel of moonlight whereby wisdom from the unconscious treasure store can more easily reach the surface.

- As the Moon rushes towards you, you may see images of the

Moon goddess or hear her voice speaking within your head, clear and bell-like. The message may be personal or it can relate to more global issues. Some people receive the message as images or as less tangible but equally valuable impressions and feelings.

- You may wish to speak the words aloud and can use a tape recorder. Afterwards you may find your voice is richer and more authoritative as it rises from your own wise depths, amplified by the Moon mother energies.

- When the voice fades, kneel down in front of your bowl of silver water and use the mirror to direct the moonlight into the bowl so that the centre shines brilliantly.

- Through half-closed eyes, just for a second so you don't hurt your eyes, look into the bowl just outside the centre brilliance and you may be rewarded by an image, perhaps of some other place or time in full moonlight. It could be a scene that holds the key to a vital but half-buried area in your life, which could be transformed with courage and the power of the full Moon.

- If you wish, you can close and open your eyes for a second image or even a third. Remember to look outside the brilliant centre, as amplified moonlight can be very bright.

- Finally take your moonstones and drop them in the water, making an affirmation of power and determination for each.

- Leave the bowl and the moonstones in the open air until the next morning.

Use the Moon water throughout the waning and following waxing period until the next full Moon. It can be kept in crystal or silver bottles, added to bathwater, drunk, sent to someone who is sick, used in ritual or poured in a polluted place. You can also sprinkle it around the photograph of a sick person, endangered species or war- or famine-torn land. It is so powerful that you do not need to use it by moonlight.

If you want to work with other people, you can use a large bowl of water or a cauldron and each person can have a mirror and moonstones. Though in covens it is generally the high priestess who channels the Moon goddess, in an informal group you can all swirl around and you will find that the words do chime in together and a joint message is created. In the bright silver water each person can add an image to create a series of interlinked visions. You can cast moonstones in turn, reciting wishes. Record the session on a tape recorder.

Whether you work alone or with a group, before bed record your full Moon channelling in pictures as well as words in your Book of Shadows.

You may not wish to draw down the Moon every month but should nevertheless leave water in a bowl from Moon rise on the day of the full Moon, with moonstones in the water and if you wish white flowers surrounding the bowl.

The Waning Moon

Use the waning Moon for removing pain, sickness and obstacles to success and happiness; lessening negative influences, addictions and compulsions; banishing negative thoughts, grief, guilt, anxiety, the envy and malice of others and destructive anger that is best let go; gently ending relationships where there are regrets but still good will.

You can work from the day after the full Moon until the waning crescent disappears from the sky. As the Moon diminishes, so the magic will be slower to come to fruition. It is good to rest from ritual for the last days of the waning cycle, though these days are good for divination.

Waning Moon magic should not be thought of as dark or banishing magic, rather as a process of bidding farewell to what is no longer wanted or helpful. Even sad or destructive habits or relationships were once part of your life and may still have emotional hooks. The essence of ritual at this time is like setting sail gently on the evening or ebbing tide.

A Candle Ritual of Farewell

• A day or two before you carry out this ritual, soak a few Moon herbs or one or two dying leaves in a small pot of saltwater. A few grains of salt will be sufficient. Traditionally seawater was used, but this has become less popular because of increasing pollution. This is a method of purification and you may begin to sense a lessening of tension as the fear, anger or destructive influences are soaked away.

- After 24 hours, filter off the water and allow the herbs or leaves to dry naturally on mesh or a rack. After dark, pour the saltwater down an outside drain or a wastewater outlet indoors, saying: 'Moon wane, Moon drain from me [name the sorrow].'

- Follow this with a drop or two of cleansing eucalyptus oil or, if you do not have any, a few drops of lemon juice. You may find that you sleep easier after this.

- The ritual itself can take place at sunset or late in the evening when the physical waning Moon has risen. Place a flat broad-based dark candle on a deep metal tray in the centre of your altar and light it, but do not light your other altar candles. Choose a fast-burning candle made of beeswax if possible.

- Burn incense which is associated with cleansing and healing, such as myrrh or lemon.

- On a dish place your salt-infused herbs or leaves and as the candle burns, say goodbye to what it is you are casting on the waning moonlight. It does not matter if the Moon has not risen, though it can be helpful to focus on it, especially in the earlier days of the waning Moon when the disc is quite full.

- Take a few herbs or a single leaf and burn them in the flame. The salt will make the candle spark. Name what it is you are burning. Brush any ash carefully on to the tray.

- Leave the wax to melt on to the tray while you collect a pot of soil or prepare a small but deep hole in the garden.

- Then sit quietly by candlelight allowing only happy memories and thoughts to surface and making positive, if modest, plans for the future.

- When the wax is still molten, draw a small circle in the centre of it with your knife and if you wish a final symbol of any sadness. Make a cross through the circle and any symbol. Score the outline of the circle deeply so that when the wax is cool you can remove the circle easily. If there is ash from the burned herbs in the circle, so much the better.

- When the wax is cool, cut out the circle and bury it in the earth, either in the pot or in the hole in the garden, with the remaining herbs or leaves.

- Dispose of the rest of the wax in a brown paper bag with the waste and tidy your altar.

- Plant Moon herbs or flowers over the buried symbol so that new life may replace what has been shed.

If the matter is difficult or long-standing, you may need to work on subsequent waning cycles. Use progressively smaller candles and leaves.

For me the Moon is one of the most exciting aspects of night magic and the easiest to connect with, even in the centre of a town. Even a few moments looking up at the Moon can still your mind and link you with the positive energies of people in many times and places.

4

The Starry Universe

On a clear night look up and you will see the glittering jewels of the universe, the stars and constellations. Their energies can empower us and extend our spiritual horizons.

Astral travel, out-of-body spirit or mind travel, takes its name from the Roman word *astra*, which means 'star' and is just one way we can explore the celestial realms. One theory is that we can actually project our psychic selves on to the surface of a planet. Others believe that in a waking dream evoked by visualisation we can explore a world created in our minds from the spiritual energies emanated by a particular heavenly body.

I will describe a simple technique for connecting with these distant realms before I introduce my interpretation of the energies of the different heavenly bodies. This interpretation is based both on traditional star lore from a number of cultures and from my own research and experiences gained from teaching others. However, you may find that you relate to the stars and constellations in an entirely different but equally valid way.

We will work with constellations, the most significant stars within those constellations and the planets that are visible to the eye without a telescope. In this way you can relate to and absorb their psychic energies directly through the physical channels. You can use a telescope to see the visible constellations and planets more clearly and countless others beyond eye range if you wish, but initially using a telescope may make it more difficult to focus on symbolic energy work.

As you read this chapter and use some of the rituals or devise your own, note down what you have learned about the different celestial spheres in your Book of Shadows.

Star Study

If you buy a star wheel or have a star-mapping programme on your computer, you can plot which stars you will see in which direction at a particular time. Studying your own section of the night sky, you will identify the various stellar systems.

The stars you can see vary according to the place in the world from which you view them as well as the time of year. Near the equator at certain times you may see stars from the opposite hemisphere.

Before attempting star magic, spend a little time just watching the stars on clear nights and learning about the way they move. If you star-watch for just five minutes with your star identifiers, in time you will be able to recognise the major constellations and planets instantly and anticipate their position.

As the year progresses you will see that stars and constellations rise over different trees or buildings or disappear altogether, to be replaced by others. We call these stars and constellations *seasonal* and generally they can be seen for six months alternately in the two hemispheres.

Others are visible within a smaller arc and are called *circumpolar* because they are closer to one of the celestial poles. These are generally visible in one hemisphere of the world or the other and never sink below the horizon.

The Story of the Stars

There are numerous accounts of the birth of the stars. My own favourite comes from the Native American Navajo tradition, where it is told the fire god set crystals from his pouch into the dark sky. The most important was the campfire of the ancestors, the Pole Star. After arranging the stars, he created the Milky Way by scattering small crystal chips across the rest of the night sky.

Star constellations are not really self-contained groups but are particularly bright stars that give the appearance of being close together and form distinctive patterns. These patterns over the ages have been identified as animals, deities or mythological heroes and heroines.

Each of the constellations and many of the major stars have names that reflect the qualities they represent, names that vary in different cultures and ages. For example, the group of seven stars within Ursa Major, or the Great Bear, is called the Big Dipper in modern America, but the stars can also be seen as a bowl with a handle and were called the Drinking Gourd by escaping American slaves who, in the words of an old song, would follow the Drinking Gourd northwards to freedom in Canada. In the UK and other parts of northern Europe the same stars are called the Plough and further north in Scandinavia the Wain, or Wagon, the wagon of the fertility god Ing or Frey. To the Inuit, the seven stars were the hunting dogs who chased the Bear into the sky.

In this chapter I have concentrated mainly on the Classical Greek and Roman interpretations, as they have most influenced modern star lore in both the northern and southern hemispheres. However, other systems, such as the Indian Vedic tradition, Chinese astrology and that of ancient Egypt, are well worth studying if star work is an area of night magic you decide to develop.

Astronomy, too, can help you understand the mechanism behind the myths and symbols and enable you to identify more easily the planetary and stellar positions throughout the year.

Working with the Stars and Constellations

The stars are the living past. We receive their light long after it has left the star itself and so they are a good focus for escaping from the parameters of time.

One way of explaining this stellar influence is to use the analogy of the aura, the psychic energy field surrounding humans, animals, plants, crystals and places. These individual energy systems interact with the energy waves of other people and even the psychic rays emitted by heavenly bodies, for psychic energies are not limited by time or distance.

This influence has been recognised for at least 6,000 years. It was set down in the early astrological systems of the Babylonians and Sumerians. The father of magic and alchemy, Hermes Trismegistos, the semi-divine Egyptian, began his *Emerald Tablet*, the keystone of the magical arts, with the words 'As Above, so Below'. The influence of the planets, especially on our emotional lives and decision-making, is the key to astrology.

The stars have retained their importance in shamanism, especially the Pole Star. A number of Wiccan groups work with stellar energies, especially their healing powers.

The Star Goddesses

To the ancient Egyptians, the sky goddess Nut was mother of the stars. Her dark body, covered with stars, was arched over Geb the Earth god as she touched the Earth with her fingers and toes. This image was painted on tomb lids of kings and pharaohs in the hope that she would grant them rebirth. Her breast milk formed the Milky Way.

In Celtic tradition Arianrhod, the beautiful and mystical goddess of reincarnation and the full Moon, turned the silver wheel of the stars and took the souls of slain heroes and heroines to be restored.

The Constellations

Look up at the Milky Way, our own galaxy, a collection of star systems that contains about 100 billion stars. Within this we can distinguish some quite distinct constellations. The constellation patterns have appeared fixed for thousands of years because although they are all moving relative to the Sun by several miles a second, they are so far away that it takes thousands of years for us to be aware of any changes in their patterns.

The apparent yearly movement of the constellations through the sky was a significant factor in the lives of ordinary men and women in earlier times, though in fact this movement is relatively slow and it is the movement of the Earth in its orbit around the Sun that creates the impression of the turning skies.

When a significant star or constellation was observed in a particular position in the sky, people knew it was time to plant their crops or that the annual rains might be expected. For example, in the eighth century BC, the Greek poet Hesiod created a Farmers' Almanac that linked the movement of particularly bright stars to agricultural events. He said that when the star cluster the Pleiades set in the West just before sunrise, ploughing should begin, as within a short time the winter rains would begin. Equally, by knowing the time of the year it was possible for sailors and travellers to identify their positions from the stars.

Despite the fact that in industrial societies such knowledge is no longer vital (though sailors who wish to earn an ocean-going yachtmaster's certificate must still study astro-navigation in case modern navigational aids suddenly fail), traditional societies still follow the stars.

Identifying the Guardians of the Stars and Constellations

It can be helpful in your star work to visualise the guardian of each constellation and significant stars. They may appear to you as beings of pure light or, like Nut, in dark robes covered with stars. Each guardian will be different, bearing the characteristics of their particular star or constellation.

Working with star guardians is a valuable way of connecting with the unique energies of each, not only to empower yourself but also to increase your innate healing energies. These will emerge spontaneously as you become filled with star power. Star energies can also calm emotions and send answers to seemingly insoluble problems.

Star guardians may transmit wisdom into your mind as images surrounded by light, as words heard in your mind or as impressions that may permeate your dreams after star watching. With some you will feel instant affinity. Your birth constellation or its ruling planet may be one you relate closely to (*see pages 75–81*). You can also focus on a star or constellation that has energies you need at particular time in your life (*see pages 67–75*). On the whole it is best to work with no more than one guardian a night.

Working with Star Guardians

- Begin by focusing on a constellation that is particularly clear in the sky. Visualise the outline shimmering.

- Breathe in the light slowly and deeply and as you exhale it, draw the star(s) nearer in your mind's eye.

- As the radiance comes nearer you will see a figure framed against the starlight. It may seem clear or be suffused in star beams.

- Greet the figure, either mentally or out loud. You may be aware of a slight tingling feeling around your body as your psychic energy field touches the higher stellar energy field.

- You may hear the guardian speak and in time you may enter into a dialogue. Should you need the qualities of the heavenly body for yourself, another person, animal or place, you can ask and in return promise to perform a small specific practical gesture to help the Earth or her creatures. This cosmic interchange is very important to ensure sufficient positive energies circulate to meet everyone's needs.

- You can ask if you may be shown a glimpse of the star sphere. You may see crystalline palaces, other light beings and beautiful gardens. These are the way our inner imaging system is able to translate the essential beauty of the energy force.

- After a while, your concentration will fade and you should thank the guardian.

- You will become aware of other stars and constellations, but tonight do not go any further or you will become psychically overtired. Spend the evening in quiet contemplation or if it is fine sitting beneath the stars, allowing their healing and empowering energies to shower down upon you.

In time you may receive quite complex channelled messages from one or two key stellar guardians. You may learn their names or you may simply refer to them as the Guardian/Lord /Lady of . . .

Keep a page in your Book of Shadows for your work with each star or constellation. You may be inspired to paint or draw the guardian or to write poetry or stories about them.

My Special Star

The stars are my friends. When I was a little girl I used to sit on the shed roof in the back yard in the centre of Birmingham and make a wish on the first star as it rose over the corporation yard chimney stack: 'Starlight, star bright, first star that I see tonight, I wish I may I wish I might, have the wish I wish tonight.'

Over the years I have seriously overworked the first star of the night with requests for passing exams, finding lost homework, getting a boyfriend and keeping a boyfriend. I wished on the first star to lose ten pounds overnight to fit into a special dress, to find the man of my dreams, have beautiful babies, write a best-selling novel and inherit a million pounds from a long-lost relative. Some of the more sensible wishes came true.

Nowadays I have stopped wishing for handsome princes and focus more on unexpected royalty cheques to pay for urgent car repairs, or that the boiler man may finally find out what is wrong with the heating system, but the stellar magic remains. I still get that thrill on seeing the first jewel in the evening sky.

Because there is very little light on the caravan site where I try to spend as much time as possible in the summer, the stars really do form a glittering bowl in the dark sky. Sometimes I work with a constellation, but often I will pick a star and ask it to send me its light. Afterwards a small blessing or answer always comes.

One night I was on my own sitting outside the caravan at twilight. I was very unhappy because my son Bill had gone to boarding school more than 100 miles away and would only come home every fortnight. Bill really needed to attend the school as he has Asperger's syndrome, the 'little professor' condition that means he can rewrite the works of Shakespeare but not tie his shoelaces. He had been very badly bullied at local schools and the first boarding school we had tried had not worked out.

I was thinking hard of Bill and missing him when I noticed the first star had risen and was unusually bright. I did not have my star map to identify it, but I sent a message to Bill through the star and recited my childhood rhyme. I hoped Bill would be looking out of his bedroom window and that we could connect somehow through the starlight. The star seemed momentarily dazzling and I felt a sense of peace.

When I phoned Bill later in the evening he was happy and making friends for the first time in his life. He said he had been feeling homesick and had been watching the stars out of his window. Then he had known I was with him and felt much better. He had gone out of his room and said hello to another boy who was missing his mum too. Then he put the phone down because he was going to play in the boy's room. As I said, sensible star wishes can come true.

Now when I have to be away from my children I often send messages to them through the first star I see. I call it my messenger star.

Major Stars and Constellations

The following are stars and constellations that are easy to see or are especially powerful. But with exploring the galaxy, your only limits are your star map and your own creativity.

Ursa Major and Ursa Minor – the Great and Little Bear

These are northern hemisphere circumpolar stars and can be seen for most of the year. They are probably the easiest northern hemisphere constellations with which to begin.

As I said earlier, the Great Bear contains the famous Big Dipper group of stars, while the Little Bear has its own Little Dipper.

Look also for the apparently nearby constellation of the *Canes Venatici*, the Hunting Dogs, two very bright stars that are pursuing the Great Bear.

Roman myth tells that Callisto was one of the maiden priestesses of the huntress and Moon goddess Diana. The supreme god Jupiter wanted her and so took the form of Diana to lure her to him. Then he turned back into his own shape and raped her. As a result, Arcas (whose name means Little Bear) was born. Juno, Jupiter's wife, was furious and made Callisto walk the Earth as a bear. Arcas grew up and while hunting was about to shoot a bear, in fact his mother. Jupiter, in a rare fit of conscience, stopped him and turned Arcas into a bear also, placing mother and son in the heavens where they might be together.

Invoke the Ursa or Bear constellation energies for courage, for protection from predators, psychological as well as physical, and for any maternal/child issues in your life.

The Ursa Major guardian is a huntress with silver arrows, dressed in shimmering silver. She is especially protective of mothers, children, young women and anyone who has suffered physical or emotional abuse.

The Ursa Minor guardian is a young hunter, never still, eager to help and full of good ideas for expanding your horizons. He works especially well for younger men and all travellers or those who seek new career horizons.

Polaris

This is the current North Pole star. It lies between the Big Dipper and the constellation of Cassiopeia. Though it seems motionless and the hub of the other constellations, it is slowly moving closer towards the celestial pole. Over the millennia, as the Earth moves in space, Polaris will move out of alignment with the North Pole but it will remain a guide for us for many centuries yet. (There is not currently a South Pole star.)

It is worth spending a little time locating Polaris, as it is the most significant star magically as well as navigationally. It marks the top of the symbolic world tree, the axis of the world. Shamans of many cultures in the northern hemisphere use it as a focus as they ascend the world tree on their astral journeys to visit the upper realms and the wise ancestors.

Mythologically, the Pole Star is associated with a number of goddesses. For example, Ethiniu, the mother of Lugh, the young Celtic god of light, was the goddess of the north star and sat in her glass tower in the night sky in silence, overseeing the events of fate and of humanity.

Invoke Polaris's energies for guidance when you feel you have lost direction emotionally or on your life path. Seek it also on astral journeys when you use the world tree as a focus, looking at the Pole Star through the branches of a tall tree. Use it to fulfil dreams and ambitions, especially those that seem hard or far off.

The Polaris guardian sits motionless on her silver throne as the stars revolve around her. She is quite misty with a crown of ice, sparkling with stellar snowflakes. But she has a warm fire you can sit beside and will help you to find your way home to the place your heart lies or give you the direction wherein such happiness may lie.

Cassiopeia

Cassiopeia is a northern hemisphere circumpolar constellation.

According to Greek mythology, Cassiopeia was a beautiful Ethiopian queen who claimed that her daughter Andromeda was lovelier than the Nereides, the nymphs of the Aegean Sea who were powerful shapeshifters and would drive insane any who perceived them under a full Moon.

To avenge the nymphs, Neptune sent a sea monster to destroy the coastal lands unless Andromeda was sacrificed. She was tied to a rock to be devoured by the monster but the hero Perseus rescued her, killed the beast and married her.

The myth may refer to an ancient ritual of a hero annually slaying the old king, later in myth portrayed as a monster, to win the hand of the young virgin princess and succeed to the throne. All the characters in the myth became constellations, apart from Andromeda, which is a galaxy. Cassiopeia, either for her vanity or perhaps because she represented the old Goddess religion, was placed on a throne in the skies which revolves around the Pole Star, so she hangs upside down for part of the year.

Invoke Cassiopeia when you need to challenge the status quo and to bring beauty and grace into your life or the world in which you live. When she flies upside down, use her energies to let go of the fear of the disapproval of others and to accept that there may be a price for fulfilling your dreams which may be worth paying.

Cassiopeia is tall and stately and insists that you address her formally. Nevertheless she will shelter all beneath the furs she wears because she comes from a hot land and is always cold. She will hold you tight as you whirl with her, shedding all the old blocks on your dreams and realising that it is better to try to fulfil them than accept the limitations others create around you.

Draco, the Dragon

A northern circumpolar constellation, Draco really does resemble a dragon and is a very exciting and visual constellation to work with.

Historically Draco is important as the home of the former Pole Star Thuban, which was used as orientation for the Egyptian pyramid of Khufu at Giza. Thus the Dragon was the guardian of treasure, both the treasure of the ancient pyramids and of the Pole Star, which offered, it was believed, a doorway into immortality.

Draco has strong pre-Greek associations with Tiamat, the Sumero-Babylonian goddess who as a great dragon gave birth to the universe from her menstrual blood, which flowed continuously for three years and three months.

In Greek legend the dragon, here called Ladon, guarded the golden apples of immortality that grew in the land of death until it was slain by Hercules. The constellation Hercules may be seen to the east of Draco in the summertime.

Invoke Draco's energies for conserving what is precious to you, for tapping into ancient wisdom and for giving birth to new life and directions in your life.

Draco is another powerful female constellation, though some do see her as male. Either way the guardian is a fiery creature with shooting stars for a crown. You cannot get too close, but may be offered a golden apple if you have been ill or exhausted, for Hercules did not take them all. You may also be shown your own hidden inner treasure.

Orion

Orion is a seasonal constellation seen in the northern winter skies and the southern summer skies. A giant huntsman, son of the ocean god Poseidon and the nymph Eurayle, he is followed by his two dogs and fights the bull Taurus, the constellation that shares his area of the sky. You can identify him by his belt, three brilliant stars in a straight line, and another line of stars hanging down that represents his sword.

A very male constellation, Orion was associated with the god Osiris in ancient Egypt. In Greek legend he was so great a hunter he vowed to kill every creature on Earth, so Gaea, the Earth Mother, sent a giant scorpion, now the constellation Scorpio, to destroy him. It stung him on the heel. Now they are at opposite ends of the sky so they can never fight again.

Invoke Orion for clear focus, for the drive to make your fortune and for persistence in attaining what it is you desire or need. He works for men of all ages and anyone who needs strength or the impetus to make a giant step forward.

Orion's guardian, like him, is strong and mighty, but very kind. He will be glad to let you ride on his shoulders if you are tired and will set you on the right path, armed with one of his special arrows that always reach their target.

Canis Major and Canis Minor

These are seasonal constellations in the northern winter skies and the southern summer skies. They are the hunting dogs who follow Orion. Canis Major contains the brightest star in the sky, Sirius, the Dog star (*see below*).

Invoke the Canis constellations if you are experiencing problems with the fidelity of others, or if your loyalty to people or causes is being tested.

The guardians of the canine constellations can be either male or female, but will waste few words, offering practical nourishment and comfort so that you feel you are supported in any endeavour. If you have any loyalty issues yourself, you will be shown where your priorities truly lie.

Sirius, the Dog Star

Sirius forms the nose of Canis Major (*see above*). It was called Sothis by the ancient Egyptians and was the most significant star in Egyptian mythology, marking the flooding of the land and the rebirth of Osiris, the Earth god who became the god of the Underworld, a supreme father god and symbol of immortal life. It was believed that the power of Sothis caused the Nile to flood each year, restoring fertility to the land. The star became identified with Isis, for it was said that her tears caused the original flooding when she heard her husband Osiris had been brutally murdered.

The first day of the Egyptian new year was celebrated in July, when Sirius could first be seen before dawn after 70 days of being hidden by the Sun's light.

To many native tribes in North America, Sirius was known as the Wolf star and the Milky Way was called the wolf trail to the heavens.

Invoke Sirius for rebirth and regeneration in your life and for extra power, emotional warmth and inspiration. It is especially helpful if you have undergone a period of spiritual or emotional darkness.

The guardian of Sirius or Sothis is a high priestess of mother Isis, her skin burnished by the Sun and totally translucent. She is very wise and compassionate, sharing your sorrows and lifting your burdens, promising that better times are ahead if you keep faith with yourself.

Sirius B

Almost as important magically as Sirius is the much smaller but very dense Sirius B, which is a companion star to Sirius. This can only be seen through a powerful telescope and is the only star I would recommend you look at initially through a telescope. Thereafter you can visualise it next to Sirius.

This tiny star is linked with the Dogon people of Mali in West Africa, who have detailed and accurate knowledge of it. They claim that this was given to them thousands of years earlier by the Nommos who came from the skies in what some claim was a spacecraft. The Nommos were described as semi-amphibious beings, resembling in part dolphins, who were sent from the Sirius star system to help humankind. It is believed that dolphins and whales are descendants of the Sirians and are the true caretakers of the Earth, since humans have abdicated this role.

Some also believe that Sirian souls still manifest in human bodies in order to help other humans and have passed on their own genes to help us to evolve. If all this seems fanciful and not possible, certainly in terms of present astronomical knowledge, you can still work with Sirian B energies as gentle healing dolphin powers.

Invoke Sirius B energies for the healing of people, animals and places, especially the oceans and their creatures. Use them also to increase your own telepathic and psychic abilities and to expand your spiritual horizons.

The guardian of Sirius B is surrounded by an aura of blue healing rays. Some visualise the guardian swimming in an azure blue sea surrounded by sea creatures or in a crystalline palace close to the sea. Playing dolphin music through a headset can help to make connection. The guardian will remind you of your responsibilities as a caretaker of the Earth and in return will help to awaken your own powers as a healer.

The Southern Cross

The Cross or Crux, a circumpolar constellation, is the most significant and easily identifiable constellation in the southern hemisphere, though it is very small. Once part of the constellation Centaurus, the Centaur, which surrounds it on three sides, the starry cross was recognised as a constellation in its own right during the 16th century. Since there is no South Pole star, Crux points the way south in the southern hemisphere.

Australian Aboriginal myth tells how Balame the All Father created two men and a woman and gave them many plants to eat. But when drought came, one of the men killed a kangaroo and he and the woman ate some of the meat. The second man refused to eat a fellow creature and travelled for many days searching for plants. At last he died beneath a huge white gum tree.

The black god of death placed the dead man in the hollow trunk and lifted the tree into the southern skies. The tree flew until it finally stopped close to the Milky Way. From it may be seen four eyes of fire, two belonging to the god and two to the first man to die. It is said that we will all go to the white gum tree in the sky one day.

Invoke the Southern Cross for overcoming fears of mortality and loss, for guidance on the meaning of life, for increased religious understanding and for protection against psychic attack.

The guardian of the Southern Cross is a highly evolved being who speaks to the heart and soul rather than the mind. He radiates gentle shimmering starlight that drives away any malevolence or negativity. He promises that if we look up to the stars we will know that our spirits will live for ever.

Centaurus, the Centaur

Centaurus, a circumpolar constellation, is one of the largest and most important constellations in the southern skies. It is associated with two centaurs, half men, half horse, Pholos and Chiron.

Chiron is perhaps the more significant centaur, not least because of the healing energies which are associated with the new distant planet with the same name. Chiron is credited with the creation of the myths of the constellations as well as with teaching astronomy, medicine and music. His pupils included the healing deity Aesculapius (*see page 134*), who became the constellation Ophiuchus, and the hero Hercules.

Pholos was killed and Chiron wounded by poisoned arrows that Hercules released when a fight broke out among the centaurs after Hercules introduced alcohol to them in spite of Pholos's warning. The immortal Chiron was left in agony, but Prometheus, the creator of mortals, took Chiron's immortality and Zeus placed him in the heavens.

Centaurus is also famed for its triple star, Alpha Centauri, the third brightest star in the sky and the closest to the Sun.

Invoke Centaurus's energies for healing old sorrows, especially of the soul or of childhood, for developing healing powers, for better understanding of star wisdom and for learning ancient secrets through divination.

The guardian of Centaurus may be in magnificent centaur form or you may see him as a wise teacher, playing a lyre beneath a tree. Listen to his words and allow them to bear fruit in your mind. You may not be aware of how much you have learned from him until you find yourself recounting unfamiliar myths or speaking of astronomical lore you have not studied.

The Pleiades

The Pleiades are a group of stars within the seasonal constellation Taurus, which is visible in the northern hemisphere winter skies and in the southern summer skies. The seven main stars have assumed great magical significance. There are in fact many more in the cluster, but seven are prominent, though only six can usually be seen without a telescope.

Recognised by sky watchers from early times, the seven stars were, according to the Greeks, seven sisters, daughters of Atlas and Pleione, who were changed into white doves by Zeus and flew into the heavens to avoid the pursuit of amorous Orion. Ironically, in the northern winter skies Orion continues to chase them.

In some philosophies the gentle sisters are married to the seven stars in the Great Bear, thus harmonising male and female energies.

The Mayan peoples consider the Pleiades to be the first seeds planted at the time of creation. Some myths recount that the Mayans themselves came from the Pleiades and were guardians of the solar system.

Invoke the Pleiades for the manifestation of thoughts and ideas, for gentle love and nurturing, for increased intuitive awareness and for harmony with the cosmos.

The guardian of the Pleiades is so gentle and ethereal she may appear transparent. However, she is a powerful source of healing for our planet and an endower of psychic wisdom. She will teach you secret rituals to help bring about your desires, as long as they are primarily for the good of others. Sometimes you may meet one of the other sisters.

Zodiacal Constellations

These seasonal constellations are best known as our astrological birth signs, though they are not necessarily the easiest to see in the sky. You can work not only with your own birth constellation but also with any whose strengths you need.

The word 'zodiac' is derived from the Greek *zodiakos kyrklos*, 'the circle of small animals'. Astrological knowledge filtered to ancient Greece around 600 BC from Mesopotamia, where certain constellations were first pictured as animal forms.

As the Earth moves around the Sun on its year-long journey, it seems that the constellations of the zodiac change their positions. For example, in the northern hemisphere, at midnight in December, Gemini is high in the sky; by March at the same time Virgo appears in that position.

Work with the actual constellation positions as you see them in the sky and with the planets you see passing through them. This coincides with the information used in the daily horoscopes you read in newspapers.

♈ Aries

The Ram
21 March–20 April
A northern winter and a southern summer constellation
Ruler Mars

The magical golden ram carried the children of King Cadmus of Thebes on its back through the air after their stepmother Ino plotted their death. Helle fell off its back and drowned, but Phrixus reached the land of Colchis safely and sacrificed the ram in gratitude to Zeus. Jason and his Argonauts sought the Golden Fleece.

Invoke Aries for assertiveness, innovation, strengthening your identity, energy and self-preservation under threat.

The Aries guardian is dressed in gold with horns of fire and may seem impatient but is helpful when you face danger or strive to achieve a worthwhile goal.

Taurus

The Bull
21 April–21 May
A northern winter and southern summer constellation
Ruler Venus

Taurus is usually identified as the white bull whose form Zeus assumed when he carried away Europa over the sea to Crete. As a result of the abduction Europa had three children, one of whom was Minos, King of Crete, whose queen Pasiphae gave birth to the Minotaur, half man, half bull, killed by Theseus.

Invoke Taurus for patience, stability, loyalty, material security and increased beauty in your life.

The Taurus guardian is surprisingly graceful, dressed in white skins. She will help you to work practically to achieve your goals.

Gemini

The Heavenly Twins
22 May–21 June
A northern winter and southern summer constellation
Ruler Mercury

There were in fact two sets of twins, both born to Leda, who was seduced by Zeus disguised as a swan. She conceived twins by him while she was pregnant by her husband, King Tyndareus of Sparta. She gave birth to two identical swan's eggs that hatched into the semi-divine twins Pollux and Helen and human twins Clytemnestra and Castor. The boys were totally devoted and when Castor was killed, Pollux persuaded Zeus to allow them to live in the sky together as the heavenly twins.

Invoke Gemini for adaptability, increased communicative powers, intellectual ability, scientific/technological acumen and versatility.

Gemini has, not surprisingly, identical twin guardians who are quicksilver and eager to be away. However, they will shower you with information and expertise you can develop at your leisure.

 ## Cancer

The Crab
22 June–22 July
A northern spring and southern autumn constellation
Ruler The Moon

This gigantic crab was sent by the goddess Hera, wife of Zeus, to hinder Hercules as he attempted to kill the sea monster Hydra. Hercules crushed the crab and so Hera placed it in the stars as a reward for his efforts.

The crab can be quite difficult to see in the sky, as some of its stars are quite faint. Locate the two claws and trace around the outline of the body.

Invoke Cancer to bring kindness and domestic happiness into your life, to attract mothering/nurturing or to increase your own, to find emotional security and to keep secrets.

The Cancer guardian may seem quite remote and formidable, but if you persist she will mellow and understand a great deal about your needs without being told.

Leo

The Lion
23 July–23 August
A northern spring and southern autumn constellation
Ruler The Sun

The lion of the constellation was the one which Hercules fought as his first task, because it was destroying the population of Nemea. Because its skin was impenetrable, Hercules choked the lion and wore the skin as armour in his future battles. To commemorate this fierce battle and the courage of the lion, Zeus placed it in the stars.

Invoke Leo for courage, leadership qualities, generosity and nobility of spirit, and to attract loyalty in others.

The Leo guardian is a true king or mighty leader, but if you are brave and address him directly, he will admire your spirit and help you find your own higher path.

♍ *Virgo*

The Maiden
24 August–22 September
A northern spring and southern autumn constellation
Ruler Mercury

Virgo is the archetypal virgin who gives her heart and soul to no man. One character associated with her is Dike, known also as the Greek goddess Tyche, a personification of justice. Others have associated her with Persephone, Greek virgin goddess of the annual rebirth of the grain, who was abducted by the Underworld god Hades and so spent winter beneath the earth.

Invoke Virgo when you need to sort your affairs and become more methodical, for integrity in self and others, for healing powers and when striving for perfection in any sphere.

Her guardian may be clad in the greens and browns of the earth and she may seem detached. Her honesty and gentle words will uplift you and help you to strive for what is of worth.

♎ *Libra*

The Scales
23 September–23 October
A northern summer constellation and a southern winter constellation
Ruler Venus

In ancient Greece Libra was part of Scorpio, representing the two claws of the scorpion. It became a constellation in Roman times to mark the balance in the year at the Autumn Equinox of equal day and night. The scales in the sky are close to the hand of Virgo, as an aspect of her role as a goddess of justice.

Invoke Libra for peace and balance in your life, especially if you are at the point of change, for peace-making and diplomacy globally as well as personally, and for justice.

Libra's guardian is veiled, but her words speak of the need for inner harmony, for we cannot react in a balanced way if external events affect our equilibrium.

Scorpio

The Scorpion
24 October–22 November
A northern summer and southern winter constellation
Ruler Mars is the ancient ruler, now co-ruler with Pluto

I have already told the story of the scorpion being killed by Hercules. However, the scorpion is also associated with the serpent at the Fall of Adam, stinging the heel of the constellation Virgo, representing Eve, who seeks to crush the serpent. This was before Libra was placed between them in the zodiac.

Invoke Scorpio for increasing psychic and mystical powers, for a sense of purpose and connection and for regeneration. Avoid it for matters of justice (work with Libra or Jupiter, *see page 85*), since the vengeance aspect can creep in.

Scorpio's guardian is a challenger of preconceived ideas and beliefs and is one to meet when you need to break a period of inertia or stagnation. But expect to be asked questions that may involve self-searching.

Sagittarius

The Archer
23 November–21 December
A northern summer and a southern winter constellation
Ruler Jupiter

Sagittarius is a very active centaur, unlike the statesman-like Chiron. He shoots his arrow towards the Scorpion in the sky. He is called Crotus, is the son of Pan and, like his father, loves the forests and hunting. However, through the influence of his mother Eupheme, nurse to the Muses who were his playfellows, he became a skilled artist and poet.

His huge constellation can be quite dim, but you can make out his form in the centre.

Invoke him for breadth of vision, honesty, open-mindedness, optimism and all artistic and creative ventures.

You will find his guardian in the wild wood, perhaps playing a pipe like the god Pan. You may have to walk fast to keep up with him. But do your best, for he will show you wondrous sights that will expand the horizons of possibility in your life.

 ## Capricorn

The Goat
22 December–20 January
A northern autumn and a southern spring constellation
Ruler Saturn

Capricornus is a sea goat, with horns and a fish tail. He is identified with Pan, the Graeco-Roman horned god of the forests and lord of the animals. Capricornus is said to have gained his fish tail when he leapt into the Nile to escape from the hot desert wind god Typhon. The constellation is held to be the portal of the gods, through which dead souls passed.

As it is quite a dim constellation, once you have identified the area in the sky, visualise the sea goat and the doorway to the stars.

Invoke Capricorn when you need to cultivate wise caution, persistence and self-discipline and to uphold or revive traditions that have been eroded.

Your Capricorn guardian may appear as an old goat herd, living as a hermit on a wild mountainside. He may talk almost to himself but his words will speak uniquely to you and awake distant memories of your ancestral heritage.

≈≈ Aquarius

The Water Carrier
21 January–18 February
A northern autumn and a southern spring constellation
Ruler Saturn is the ancient ruler, now co-ruler with Uranus

Aquarius is a handsome youth called Ganymede whom Zeus appointed as the deities' cup bearer in the place of Hera's daughter Hebe; he is frequently depicted with a jug in either hand. Aquarius's double stream of water became associated in medieval alchemy with mystical life-giving dew.

Invoke Aquarius for independence, idealism, inventiveness, innovation, emotional detachment and humanitarian projects.

At the place where a stream divides in two you may find the guardian of Aquarius pouring water with one hand and drawing it out with the other. You may be allowed to drink from these waters of wisdom and knowledge. Do not take too much or you will not be invited again.

 ### *Pisces*

The Fish
19 February–20 March
A northern autumn and southern spring constellation
Ruler Jupiter is the ancient ruler, now co-ruler with Neptune

The two fish of Pisces swimming in opposite directions represent the fish that saved Aphrodite and Eros, the Greek mother and son deities of love, when they leapt into the River Euphrates to escape Typhon, who was creating a storm. The gods placed the fish in the heavens to show their gratitude.

Unlike the astrological glyph of the fish swimming in opposite directions, in the sky you will see the two fish joined at the tails and hanging downwards.

Invoke Pisces's energies to increase your sensitivity, sympathy and empathy with others (and theirs with you), as well as imagination, intuition and spiritual development.

The guardian of Pisces is dressed in sea greens and blues and will be found on the seashore. She will share your sorrows and joys and will help you to flow with life rather than be submerged.

The Planets

Planets have always been recognised as having especially powerful auras that interact with the human psyche and also that of places. In this way, they can impart certain qualities and strengths to people, especially to those whose birth signs they rule or reside in at the moment of birth.

In the view of many modern astrologers, rather than planetary movements *causing* earthly changes, cosmic and mundane events occur simultaneously, but are linked through what Jung called *synchronicity* or *meaningful coincidence*.

Unlike the constellations of the zodiac, which appeared to ancient astrologers to circle the Earth in a regular pattern, the planets follow their own orbits around the Sun. The word 'planet' comes from the Greek word for 'wanderer'.

If you use an astrological diary, an ephemeris or a journal like *Old Moore's Almanac,* you can find out which planets are moving into which of the 12 zodiacal constellations and whether any are retrograde, i.e. apparently moving backwards and thus slowing down matters, generating confusion and unfocused energies. You can then use your computer program to plot exactly where the planets are in the sky.

As with constellations, work directly with the planets by drawing down their energies rather than trying to plot their relationships to others in the sky, as that is the province of astrology.

Planets are much brighter than the majority of stars, but their identifying characteristic is that they appear as a constant point of light as compared with the twinkle of stars.

You can identify five planets with the naked eye: Mercury, Venus, Mars, Jupiter and Saturn. You will not necessarily see them all at the same time.

You can work with the energies of the more distant planets that are not visible without a telescope, but as with the stars, I have concentrated here on those that you can relate to directly.

☿ Mercury

Mercury is the smallest planet and as the one closest to the Sun is the fastest in its orbit. Mercury was named after the Roman winged messenger of the gods, known as Hermes to the Greeks. He was the son of Jupiter. Carrying a rod entwined with two serpents that could induce sleep and healing, he travelled as messenger between the heavens, Earth and the Underworld. Through his skill and dexterity, communicative abilities and quicksilver mind, Mercury came to rule over commerce and medicine, and in the modern world science and technology.

You may need to be patient to see Mercury because he is so close to the Sun. However, there are times throughout the year when he can be seen clearly at twilight or just before dawn. It is worth using an astronomical website to identify these periods well in advance so that you can mark them in your Book of Shadows for Mercury work. You will see the planet physically as orange, except when it is low in the sky, when it will radiate flashes of rainbow colours.

Whenever you need Mercurial energies in your life you can focus on the constellation he is passing through (a speedy business, as he takes only 88 days to whiz around the entire 12 signs of the zodiac). Visualise the silver-winged messenger within a sphere of brilliance set against the constellation (which itself may not be visible at certain times of the year).

Invoke Mercury for all matters concerned with learning, for using logic if you are being swamped by emotion, for clear communication, for healing self, others, animals and the planet, for urgent financial needs and to launch new projects, for short-distance house moves and new careers.

Visualise the guardian of Mercury in swirls of coloured smoke surrounded by herbs and potions, crystals and gleaming phials of jewel-coloured healing liquids, writing in huge books in strange writing. He is ageless, in some lights an earnest young scientist, in others one of the ancient alchemists who have spent a lifetime in study. Ask and you will not be given solutions but taught how to find your own answers.

♀ Venus

Venus is sometimes known as the morning or evening star, because she shines with a brilliant silvery hue and can be seen most clearly at these times. At her brightest she is the most brilliant object in the sky apart from the Sun and Moon.

Venus, whose Greek name was Aphrodite (born of the foam), was beauty incarnate, the Roman goddess of birth, love, beauty, the arts, grace and possessions that we value as expressing our essential self. This is the Venus you see just before dawn. In her evening aspect, however, Venus was a warrior goddess and represents female power and the role of fate in our lives.

Check with a sky program when Venus is visible, as when she disappears from the evening sky she will not reappear in the morning for a few months. However, once she leaves the early morning sky, she will soon reappear at twilight.

When you cannot see her, visualise her in her current constellation (check a Moon diary or ephemeris) as a flowing woman of silver in a gown studded with emeralds and pearls. If you are seeking her power side, look for her as a warrior woman in shining armour with a jewel-encrusted sword and a single diamond for a helmet. Slower than Mercury, she takes 225 days to travel through all the constellations.

Invoke Venus for all environmental matters, the arts, for love, fidelity in relationships, for fertility, for bringing beauty into your life, for the positive increase of female authority and power in fighting inequality or violence against women.

The guardian of Venus is dazzlingly beautiful but not at all vain. She is compassionate and will help you to preserve the environment. Above all, she will help you to value inner grace and beauty as much as outer form.

♂ Mars

Mars is the planet with a reddish tinge – red being seen as a warlike colour, it was named after the Roman god of war, Ares to the Greeks. Mars, son of Jupiter, was the father of Romulus and Remus, who founded Rome, and as god of both agriculture and war, represented the ideal Roman as farmer and conqueror of new lands.

Mars represents initiative, independent action and maintaining a positive sense of identity and self-confidence. As well as his innate quality of courage, at his most positive Mars can display a nobility of spirit, when anger and warlike impulses are directed against injustice and inertia.

The actual planet is best seen for a short period that occurs every two years when its orbit comes closer to Earth and so is more visible as well as much brighter, temporarily more dazzling even than Jupiter. What is more, every 18 years, at its point of nearest contact to Earth, its psychic vibrations are very strong. Check an astronomical program or journal for precise dates.

When you cannot see Mars clearly, visualise a powerful leader, clad in red, riding his burnished gold chariot across the current constellation. He takes nearly two years to span the zodiac, so has time to bring change for those born in the constellation he is visiting.

Invoke Mars in his most positive aspects for the energy and determination to make positive change, for overcoming seemingly insurmountable obstacles by sheer determination and for the refusal to be deterred. Call him, too, as a powerful negotiator and as an antidote to violence, terrorism and brutal regimes that use repression to crush the will of others. Above all, use his power and courage as a liberator to free yourself from old restrictions, fears and controls.

The guardian of Mars is clearly a leader in his scarlet robes, talking with ambassadors while horses whinny in the courtyard, eager to be away. He will tell you what you need to know in a few stirring words that may seem more like a call to battle. Listen carefully, for he will not repeat himself. But his message holds the key to defeating your inner or outer dragons.

4 *Jupiter*

Jupiter, the largest planet, is for much of the time the second brightest planet in the sky, shining creamy white.

He is very visible for continuous expanses of time. Jupiter, known as the Sky Father, was the supreme Roman god, ruler of the universe. Like his Greek counterpart Zeus, he controlled the thunderbolts, which were carried by his eagle, the king of the birds.

Jupiter is regarded as the most benevolent and wise of the planetary rulers. Indeed, he is known as the joy-bringer and is associated with all forms of good fortune and prosperity, with ideals and altruism, higher values, wisdom through experience, learning, expansiveness and increase of what you have already created. He brings justice, and earthly and spiritual authority.

If you cannot see Jupiter in the sky, you have plenty of time to visualise him in each constellation, as he takes about 12 years to circle the zodiac, so spends a year in each sign. Picture him with a huge wreath of stars, dressed in imperial purple with an orb and sceptre in his hand, extending his arms wide to invite all to share his banquet and listen to his oratory.

Invoke Jupiter for the acquisition of knowledge, for easing all dealings with authority and recourse to justice, for rising above pettiness or spite, for taking a long-term perspective on life and events, for major career or long-distance house moves or improvements, for good health and for leadership qualities.

The guardian of Jupiter is regal but will never turn away someone who is willing to cast off illusion and pretensions. He will give you the gift of power but weld responsibility to it and seek pledges that it will be used for the good of others.

♄ Saturn

Saturn is the second largest planet and is surrounded by rings. These cannot be seen by the naked eye. He can appear slightly yellow, though he is as bright as the brightest star. In mythology, Saturnus, the Roman form of Cronus, god of time, was Jupiter's father. He was deposed by his son after he had devoured all his children except Jupiter, Neptune, god of the sea, and Pluto, Lord of the Underworld. Saturnus was sent to Italy, where he taught agriculture and engineering, and established a Golden Age of peace and abundance.

As the shadow side of Jupiter, Saturn is the reality factor, bringing the constraints of fate, time and space. However, he can transform obstacles into opportunity by stimulating effort and perseverance. Saturn's strengths are in his persistence. In adversity, he has endless patience, tolerance and guardianship of inner mysteries and secrets that are acquired over years rather than weeks. With Saturn we can also work unafraid with our own shadow, allowing what we have tidied away out of sight to be released and utilised or discarded.

You can easily see Saturn when he is in the sky, but when he is out of sight for a long period, you can visualise him in the current constellation. Because he takes 28–30 years to complete his orbit of the zodiac, he will spend more than two and a half years in each sign. Visualise him as Old Father Time with a white flowing beard and grey robes, holding the globe in his right hand.

Invoke Saturn, the father of night magic, for developing your psychic and spiritual nature, for all worries concerning ageing and mortality, for help with animals, the home, money or property. He will also make it easier to operate within constraints to achieve step-by-step realistic aims.

Your Saturn guardian, who may be male or female, will be in a library with many dusty books or an observatory looking out at the stars. The guardian will be very old and largely silent. But each word will be a jewel of wisdom to be examined and treasured and hopefully made part of a collection gathered over time.

Working with the Starry Sky

Much star wisdom and energy will come through focusing on or visualising a particular star, constellation or planet, gently breathing in its light and talking to the guardian.

Over the months and years you may create a particular ritual or invocation for your favourite heavenly bodies. The following is just one suggestion. It is especially effective at a seashore or in an open space and is useful for drawing the energy of the stars into yourself.

Drawing Down the Stars

- Draw a waist-high circle with a large outdoor incense torch that you can leave burning in the centre of the circle, either in a tall container or wedged in the ground with stones.

- Within the smoke circle, face the four directions in turn, beginning with the North.

- Extend your magic wand or crystal in each direction, then point it downwards to the earth and finally upwards towards the chosen star or constellation.

- As you do so, ask the blessing and protection of each of the four guardians of the directional watchtowers and of Mother Earth while you work.

- Finally call the star's name and ask that you might see the guardian or the realm in your mind's eye and receive the guardian's blessings.

- Sit or lie on a mat in the centre of the circle if you wish and establish contact by breathing in the starlight (*see pages 64–5*). Some people create their smoke circle around a rock or tree stump as a seat for visualisation work.

- Draw the star around you and step gently on to the surface. Ask permission of the guardian to remain and each time you visit see if you can explore more of the realm.

- Afterwards thank the star guardian, the Earth and the four guardians of the directions.

• Extinguish any remaining incense in a bowl of sand.

Keep a record of these rituals. You may channel wisdom from the guardian or this may follow in your dreams.

On pages 139–40 I have described a method of astral travel you can adapt to reach your chosen stellar destination. This may give you richer and more detailed experiences than visualisation. However, sometimes you will just want to stand beneath the starry heavens and marvel at their splendour.

I have gained so many gifts and strengths from the stars, perhaps the most important being the patience and perseverance of Saturn. He has steadied me so many times when I have wanted to be off on an adventure my bank tells me I cannot afford until 2025 at the earliest, though sometimes Mercury has shown me a short cut. Saturn gives me the staying power to revise a book, to fill in forms, not to let money burn a hole in my pocket and to say no (occasionally) to my children. His grandfatherly wisdom ensures that I do not fall out of my canoe as I paddle furiously across the turbulent waters of being outwardly a working mother of five, but at heart a gypsy dreamer. You will find your missing qualities too if you look upwards and let your soul soar.

5

The Power of Winter

I visited Moscow in December 20 years ago. It was bitingly cold, dry with burning ice and banks of whiteness so deep that little children and dogs dived into the drifts and momentarily disappeared. Crone goddesses were everywhere, muffled in their black woollen scarves and long coats, sweeping paths in the snow around the ice rink in Gorky Park and round the Eternal Flame. In Red Square they waited patiently in the cold hour after hour to visit Lenin's tomb, not stamping their feet, blowing their fingers or complaining, but statue still, icons of the winter and of the dignity of age.

I saw a procession of wise women in Zagorsk, the seat of the Russian Orthodox Church, their lips moving silently as they recited age-old words in the dimly lit gold-orbed churches clustered around the square before dragging their sledges of provisions or logs homewards across the ice.

Snow was everywhere, falling as swiftly as it was cleared, blanketing the apartment blocks and the fields where old women were tending the scraggy animals. With the same stoical unsentimental compassion they carried their infant grandchildren swaddled on their backs or helped them stumble homewards through the black and white darkness.

I did not know of magic then, but I instinctively knew these old women were the rulers of the winter, the grandmothers about whom I had read in fairy stories, Mother Russia who had set her face against so many storms over so many years. Their eyes showed neither resentment nor anger. Winter was to be endured, because it was winter. They are there still. When I write about winter magic, I think of them and make my offerings to their silent courage and their total immersion in the energies of the season.

The Season of Winter

Because of the tilt of the Earth's axis, the seasons in the northern hemisphere are the opposite of those in the southern hemisphere. Thus, like day and night, winter and summer revolve in a continuous cycle around the Earth. Magically, too, the cycle of the seasons reflects different energies, each of which has equal value and significance.

Many of the older calendars divided the year into only two seasons, summer and winter, corresponding to the dark and light halves of the year. Our ancestors recognised the importance of using the darker days and longer nights for spiritual as well as physical rest and regeneration. But they also knew that when darkness and cold reached their peak, so light and warmth stirred anew. It is no accident that in a number of cultures festivals of rebirth and abundance take place in deepest winter.

Winter rituals can help us to work with the energies of dark times of the year to develop our rich inner world, to let go of what is no longer needed and to create abundance and light in our lives at times of actual or spiritual cold.

Harsher weather can also serve as a catalyst for rituals of transformation and inner power. We can use driving snow, rain, wind or thunder to clear away what is redundant and to rekindle our own inner resilience and powers of regeneration.

You will find winter rituals helpful not only during the winter months but also at times when you need to slow down your pace. They will re-establish your connection with your inner world when daily life becomes fraught or frantic.

First come the true winter rituals of welcoming the slower rhythms of the darker, colder days, of returning to the fireside to wait and grow strong within, and letting the fields lie fallow.

Slowing the pace and reconnecting with these slower, more natural energies is one of the most healing aspects of winter rituals.

Myths of Winter

If we look at some of the myths of winter in different cultures it is possible to understand the principles behind traditional winter rituals and so to adapt them to the modern world.

Celtic

The Celts perhaps more than any other people were aware that darkness and light were equally necessary and so began their year as darkness increased at Samhain, the first evening of which is now called Halloween.

The Celts used the symbolism of dark and light brother gods who fought for supremacy at the Equinoxes, the balance points of equal day and night. Each god died and was reborn annually and each ruled for half the year in a continuing cycle.

The light god brother defeated darkness at the Spring Equinox around 21 March. This heralded increasing light and warmth. At this festival the light god won the right to impregnate the Earth Mother. This ensured his successor would be born at the Midwinter Solstice, around 21 December, the height of the dark god's power but also the beginning of his decline as the days began to get longer.

The dark god gained supremacy at the Autumn Equinox around 21 September and impregnated the Goddess so that his successor would be born at the Summer Solstice around 21 June, the height of the light god's power but also the beginning of his decline as the nights became progressively longer.

In the southern hemisphere the dates move around six months. The names and details change, but that is the rationale of the myth. So the Midwinter Solstice magically represents rebirth and regeneration, both spiritually and in our everyday world.

Ancient Greek and Roman

In the ancient Greek and Roman worlds it is the Earth Mother who brings winter. Demeter, the Greek goddess of the grain and harvest, brought about the first winter as she mourned the abduction of her daughter Persephone by Hades, god of the Underworld. Through the intervention of the father god Zeus, Persephone was returned to the world. However, because she had eaten pomegranate seeds in the Underworld, she had to live there for four months each year. This heralded winter, when her mother again grieved.

This cycle was intimately linked with the Eleusian Mysteries. The mystery religions that reached their height in the ancient Greek world were secret rites that were often performed deep in caves in the womb of the Earth Mother. By sacred song, dance and sexual ceremonies, they ensured the fertility of the land and passed on to initiates the secret knowledge of the Great Goddess herself.

The central tenet of the Demeter/Persephone myth seems to have been that just as grain returns every spring after its harvest and wintry death, so the human soul is reborn after the death of the body.

So the winter holds powers of future growth and the ability to nurture and be nurtured.

Viking

In Scandinavian myths, because winter was such a long season, ice was central to creation itself and was regarded as the fifth element. Life was created from the world ice from Niflheim, the realm of cold and snow in the North, combined with the cosmic fires of Muspellheim, the realm of blazing heat and volcanoes in the South. The first being, Ymir the frost giant, emerged from an ice block.

Mother Holda, the Crone form of the mother goddess Frigg, presided over the changing weather. In her cave she cherished children who had died young or were as yet unborn. When it snowed it was said she was shaking her feather mattress.

Her husband Uller, Viler or Holler, the winter god, was known as the Dark Odin. He usurped the throne of the father god Odin, who had left the world untended after a bitter quarrel with Frigg. Uller travelled on his huge snowshoes over the frozen wastes and ruled during the winter months. But he was very mean and never gave gifts to humankind so they always welcomed the return of Odin, who drove Uller back to the frozen North at May time.

Uller covered the fields of his wife with snow during the winter to make them more fruitful when the spring came. The wintry weather was thus seen as a protective shield over the Earth, enabling it to rest and regenerate.

So winter rituals can also invoke protection and inner transformation that will be manifest as action in spring.

Working with the Crone

The most prevalent and creative symbol of winter in many cultures and ages is the Crone or wise grandmother. Though she has become the wicked witch of fairy tale, her role was originally protective.

The Crone takes many forms. In Ireland the Bean-Tighe is an Irish fairy housekeeper/grandmother who cares for mothers, children and pets, and will finish chores around the home. In Russia, they call the resident Crone Dolya. She is a tiny old fairy lady who lives behind the stove and brings good fortune.

My own favourite Crone is the Cailleach, or Veiled One, the name given to the Celtic Goddess in her winter or Crone aspect. It is likely that the cult of the Cailleach is many thousands of years old in Scotland, Ireland, Wales, France and England, far predating the Celts.

Associated with cairns and standing stones, which some believe were created as part of her early worship, the Cailleach was reborn at Halloween, the beginning of the Celtic winter and New Year. She travelled through the land, striking the earth with her staff, on which a crow perched, and calling down the snow so that the soil might rest and grow strong again.

The Crone would also break the ice to enable the animals to drink and ensure that they had sufficient fodder. Folk tales in the Scottish Highlands tell how she would knock at doors of crofts seeking shelter by the fireside on the coldest days. If welcomed, she would reward the house with good fortune and often fill the grain store so it would never empty.

On May Eve, the beginning of the Celtic summer, the Crone would throw her staff under a holly tree or a gorse bush (both were her sacred plants) and turn herself into a stone once more.

The Wisdom of the Crone

Crone magic has enjoyed a revival in recent years as older women celebrate the power that comes with experience. Younger people and men have also discovered that this gentle but potent source of wisdom is one that can give depth to ritual.

In the northern hemisphere, October, November and December, the months before the Midwinter Solstice, are the most common for Crone rituals, but you can perform them on any dark, cold day throughout the year. They are often performed on the three days before the crescent Moon is in the sky, and at the Crone's special time of twilight, but you can call on her powers at any time.

Crone rituals are a good way of building up your wisdom and regularly renewing calm and protection. They are especially associated with developing inner wisdom, patience and a still centre that allows for inner growth.

When I was younger the ghosts of old women terrified me because they seemed hostile and I would run away or hide my head beneath the bedclothes. As I grew older, I realised that it was the fact that they were old that was frightening. Once I stopped running and started listening I found that they were wise friends. Now, as I struggle with my own ageing processes, they are teaching me to look into the mirror and welcome the lines of experience and laughter and not mourn for lost youth.

Crone Symbols

In earlier times the Crone was remembered primarily by piles of stones or seasonal berries and leaves set on one of her standing stones, or by offerings left by ancient yew or elder trees, but today a new tradition is growing up.

Now she has her special crystal, a deep purple amethyst, and myrrh or cypress incense. You may like to buy a special amethyst to set in the centre of your altar for Crone work. Though the association with the amethyst has come from recent Crone ceremonies, this dark stone is one that works well for older women and so is a natural choice.

My favourite tradition is weaving a Crone circlet from holly without berries, winter flowers and twigs that have lost their leaves, mingled with evergreen.

Making a Crone Circlet

• Gather the materials for your circlet before dusk.

- Weave the basic circlet from either soft pliant cane, the kind you use for weaving baskets, or pliant branches from which the thorns have been removed. Bind it with purple twine.

- Then add the leaves, flowers and twigs, using purple twine where necessary but keeping this to a minimum.

- If you are an older woman, as you work endow the circlet with all your dreams as yet unfulfilled and whisper to it the secrets of your heart.

- If you are younger or a man, focus on your mother or grand-mother and weave in your love for her and all the kindnesses she has shown you. If the relationship was bad, blend forgiveness as you work. If possible, send her some flowers or a card or take her a small gift in the near future.

- Keep your Crone circlet on the altar from the Autumn Equinox to the Spring Equinox or from the beginning to the end of the Celtic winter, from dusk at Samhain, 31 October, to 30 April, May Eve.

- Regularly replace any flowers that have died.

- For Crone rituals you can encircle the Crone amethyst.

Communicating with the Crone

You can talk to the Crone goddess by sitting at your altar, lighting a deep purple candle so it shines on her crystal and holding or wearing your circlet.

Speak as you would to a wise older person (whatever your age she will predate you by centuries) about grief, loss, concerns about ageing and mortality, lack of confidence, doubts, matters of justice, all endings. The Crone can offer protection, especially to children and animals, give you the strength and courage to overcome your fears, and remove destructive influences.

Even if you have no problems, it can be a great spiritual step forward to walk into the darkness with the Crone by the light of the single candle. One of her first challenges is: 'Will you walk into the darkness with me?'

That darkness may be an external terror, but we also all have our personal inner darkness. With the Crone's help we can learn to lose our fears and accept what lies within us.

Walking into the Darkness with the Crone

Wrap up warmly so you can work outdoors on a dark, cold moonless night or before the Moon has risen. I carried out this ritual in the garden of my Swedish publisher, with no houses or lights for miles. Work in an open flat space where there are no hazards, or a grove where the trees are evenly spaced, or best of all, you may be able to find a small ancient stone circle that will be deserted in winter and work from the centre of that. Have an electric torch in your belt or bag so you can have light if you get confused and to help you find your way back.

- Begin as dusk is falling.

- You will need four black feathers to represent the night crow, the Crone's special bird. Alternatively, use four small knotted chains of black thread.

- Draw or create a circle with small stones that is approximately ten paces from the centre at its four radii, the four compass points. Familiarise yourself with the four directions and any landmarks such as trees or large stones.

- Stand in the centre and if you wish wear your Crone circlet.

- In the fading twilight take ten paces to the North, holding your hands in front of you, slightly raised. Carry two feathers or thread chains in each hand. Say: 'I will walk into the darkness with you, Lady Crone, wise grandmother, knowing you will not let me stumble.'

- Stop and, facing outwards, say: 'I look into the outer darkness, into the depths of the winter night, knowing through it lies the summer, dawn, new light and life. I cast away one fear.'

- Name a particular fear and cast a feather into the air.

- Turn right around and take ten paces towards the centre, saying: 'I will walk into the inner darkness, with you, Lady Crone, wise grandmother, knowing you will show me what I need to know.'

- Stop and, facing inwards, say: 'I look into the inner darkness, into the depth of my soul in winter, knowing through it and within it lies the summer dawn of new light and life. I embrace one truth.'

- Wait and you may hear a voice, see an image etched in the darkness or gain some new insight or awareness.

- Walk directly ahead southwards for ten paces, repeating the words for embracing the outer darkness and casting away another fear and another feather.

- Turn and walk again to the centre for ten paces, repeating the words for embracing the inner darkness and receiving another truth from the wise Crone.

- Make a half turn clockwise so you are facing the East and repeat the outer darkness part of the ritual.

- As you return to the centre again and have embraced your third truth, walk directly ahead westwards for ten paces, cast your final feather and return to the centre for the final truth.

- Stand in the centre for a few more moments and tell the wise Crone your deepest secret desires and worries and hear her answers.

- When you are ready to leave, thank her and perhaps leave a tiny amethyst in the centre of the circle.

- Switch on your torch and walk home through the darkness with confidence.

This is a very powerful ritual, so do not be afraid if you feel the Crone touch your hand lightly.

Make notes in your Book of Shadows, so you can reread the wise advice you receive from the Crone in your rituals and refer back to the experiences on your psychic journey.

Different Ways of Meeting the Crone

Though she is goddess of the winter months and later years, you can always call on the Crone when the day is dark either physically or emotionally. If you feel totally lost, cynical and angry with yourself, others or the unfairness of life, you can seek her comfort in the following ways:

- Place an amethyst in a dark glass bowl filled with water on the floor in front of your altar, then light your purple altar candle and kneel in front of it, gazing deep into the amethyst in the water.

- Put on your Crone circlet and touch an elder, yew or another ancient tree and invoke the Crone's wisdom with either the following chant or one you devise yourself:

  Wise woman of winter, who makes the fields lie fallow so that they may grow strong, who breaks the ice for the creatures and brings straw for their byres, give me likewise, I ask, in this wintertide of the year, life, peace, nurturing and protection. Let me sit by your fireside and hear your wise words and lead me through the darkness to the light of rebirth.

- Look for the Crone in caves and recesses in rocks (*see pages 158–60*). Look into the darkness and call her name. Many of the more famous caves have legends of witches or prophetesses who were probably actual wise women healers who lived there to escape persecution.

- Call out for her near animals in a snow-covered field.

- Seek her on a windswept moorland at twilight, close to a clump of trees.

- Find her close to monoliths, single standing stones or cairns in semi-darkness or in small stone circles.

- Light a small fire in a hearth of stones in a sheltered place during the winter months and invite her to join you. Burn a few dried herbs such as sage or thyme on the fire.

- If you have an open hearth at home, you can make a Crone hearth so that the Crone will enter your home at night and bring her blessings. Make her welcome with arrangements of autumn and winter flowers, berries and a small basket of root vegetables near the hearth. She loves honey cakes too.

- Alternatively, you can make a small hearth against a wall with a border of bricks or tiles and a small cauldron-type iron pot filled with sand in which you can set a broad purple Crone candle or a pillar candle on a metal tray.

• The Crone loves to help with the garden before winter and she also welcomes an indoor herb garden or plants grown in a conservatory or a huge glass bottle.

• Leave a lamp or night-light for her on the darkest nights near your night altar and you may sense her presence when you next enter the room.

Light in the Darkness

Autumn and winter rituals are also a way of attracting prosperity and joy into your life at a time when you may feel depressed by constant rain and dark evenings or a personal run of bad luck.

The myths of the rebirth of light, the Sun god or king around the Midwinter Solstice and its accompanying festivals have been an important way of expressing the belief that new life will blossom after the winter. The fact that the days do get longer, if not warmer, after the Midwinter Solstice is affirmation that the wheel of the year is ascending once more after reaching its lowest point in mid-December in the northern hemisphere and six months later in the southern hemisphere.

Festivals of Light in Different Cultures

Some festivals of light in the darkness, especially in warmer countries, are not directly related to the Solstice. However, they echo a similar theme – that if artificial light in the form of candles, torches or firelight is introduced into the darkness, then the natural light and warmth will be kindled by a transference of power.

Diwali

Diwali, Deepawali or Divali is an autumnal Hindu festival of light. It is also celebrated by Sikhs. Deepawali means 'rows of *diyas*' (clay lamps) and oil lamps, or *diyas*, and candles illuminate every home and building at this time. Even on the waterways tiny boats of leaves or coconut shells carry lights and there are firework displays everywhere.

Diwali is celebrated 20 days after Dussehra, on the thirteenth day of the dark fortnight of the month of Asvin (October–November). It also marks the beginning of the Hindu New Year.

One of the main deities worshipped during this period is Lakshmi, the goddess of wealth and good fortune. Lights and candles are placed in windows so that Lakshmi will look in and endow prosperity upon the family, and *rangolis*, or coloured patterns, are painted on floors and walls to attract her benevolence.

Chanukah

Chanukah or Hanukkah, the Hebrew festival of light, begins on 25th Kislev, which is approximately November–December on the secular calendar, and lasts for eight days.

It commemorates the miracle in 165 BC when the Hasmoneans, or Maccabees, re-entered Jerusalem's Holy Temple, which had been defiled by Syrian invaders, and rededicated it. The Maccabees wished to rekindle the menorah, the seven-branched candelabrum, but most of the oils had been defiled and they found only one small cruse of pure oil. It was enough to burn for only one day, but it burned for eight.

In memory of the miracle of the Temple menorah, a special menorah called a Chanukiah, or Hanukkiya, was created and this is the origin of the special candelabrum used at the festival today. This is usually a nine-branched candelabrum whose candles are lit by a Shamash, or servant candle, which then takes its own place at the centre of the menorah. One candle is added each night until all eight candles are present and lit. The Chanukiah is usually placed near a window or a door so passers-by can see its light.

Method for Attracting Abundance and Prosperity

Oil-based foods are part of the feasting in memory of the miracle of the Temple oil and indeed feasting is a significant part of all festivals of light in the darkness, not least the modern Christmas. Traditionally, a feast was a magical gesture at times of the year when there was dearth.

The following ritual can be used to attract abundance and prosperity in whatever area you need it, remembering the old magical rule of enough for your needs and a little more. Though it is especially powerful on the actual Solstice day, and can be a good focal point for a group or family celebration, if you will not be spending Christmas together or hate the commercialisation of Christmas, you can adapt it for any low point in either a physical or an emotional winter.

You can work either before dawn or, my own favourite, as dusk falls on the day of the Midwinter Solstice (around 21 December, according to the calendar). Both dawn and dusk were used as marker points on Neolithic passage graves so that the shafts of rising or dying light on this day would carry the souls to rebirth.

You can also work at dusk on Solstice Eve or the nearest weekend, as many pagan groups do, so you have time to enjoy the period around the ritual and tune into the Earth's changing energies at this time of transition.

I work with the dusk because this is especially good for amplifying night energies. You can also walk into the darkness with the dying Sun in the belief that he will rise again. You can celebrate alone, with friends and family or in a more formal group.

If possible, spend the day in either a place of antiquity or one of natural beauty, gathering holly and greenery to decorate your home for Christmas. This is a wonderful antidote to pre-Christmas panic. You can also carry out the ceremony on Christmas Eve at dusk or midnight or early on Christmas morning to merge pagan and Christian traditions that are very close in essence.

- Stand preferably outdoors as the light fades, gently breathing the falling darkness. Let go into the descending night all that is redundant or did not work out.

- Visualise the Crone, sometimes accompanied by her two sisters, the Matronae or Mothers of the Night, waiting to act as midwives for the new Sun or Son of God, and know she has not deserted you on this darkest night. In the old Irish tradition St Bridget occupied this role.

- Light a lamp. You can buy ornamental ones containing a nightlight quite cheaply at hardware stores. If indoors, use a white or natural beeswax candle.

- Say: 'Mothers of this darkest night, I offer in this light, brightness to the darkness, hope to lift doubt, joy to lift despair, in faith that the Sun will be born anew and life return.'

- You can add a request for any particular rebirth that you need in your life or wish for the regeneration of a place or an endangered species.

- Project the image of renewal into the flame of the lamp.

- When it is totally dark, extinguish your lamp, making sure you know exactly where your matches and taper are. (You may wish to keep a tiny pencil torch alight.)

- If in a group, form a circle. All lights should be extinguished at the same moment. One person acts as the light keeper, holding a tiny flame from which they can light a taper that will then rekindle all the other lights.

- As you put out the light, say: 'Light to darkness, as I walk into the darkness I trust that the wheel of the year will turn and light will be reborn. I call to the Sun, arise anew.'

- Wait a few moments in this symbolic transition time and connect with the darkness before creation and the birth of the world. You may see this as swirling clouds, as deep dark water or as a pure black velvet sphere. Breathe slowly and merge with the womb of the universe.

- When you are ready, relight the lamp. In a group the lights will be ignited one by one until the circle is ablaze. Say: 'The Sun is born again. Light in the darkness, on this cold winter's day life is born again.'

- Now call to the skies for your personal rebirth or one you wish for the land or people.

- If possible, take your lighted lamp into your home, but if this is not practical, pass a taper through the flame and as it flares extinguish both, saying: 'Carry the seeds of light within to be rekindled in my home and the hearts of those I love.'

- Indoors, light as many candles or night-lights as you wish in the main living room. Use old bottles or jars if you run out of containers. You can use domestic candles that are half-burned. Make sure they are in safe places, not near electrical appliances, and do not leave them unattended. Floating candles in bowls of water are one safe solution, as are ones in glass containers buried in coloured sand.

- Decorate the room with any greenery you gathered and add silver and gold baubles or ribbons.

- Have ready a large dish or bowl covered with gold foil and filled with tiny golden-coloured or brass objects – coins, charms, crystals or glass nuggets.

- Let your Solstice lantern or a candle lit from the newly kindled Solstice taper shine on the dish of gold objects to attract abundance of every kind to your home.

- Hold a fresh taper to the Solstice light and make a long-term wish for yourself or others.

- Leave the light and taper to burn through as you eat a pre-prepared meal of golden casseroled vegetables, and meat if you wish, followed by golden and orange fruit.

- Spend the evening making music, singing carols and enjoying other forms of home entertainment. Use the Solstice light to weave images of your golden tomorrows.

Attracting Light and Abundance on the Coldest Days

- On the Solstice morn before dawn (or any other morning you need light) wait in the darkness until dawn is breaking, then light a long-lasting candle as the first light enters the sky. As the light rises, hold your flame up to it and say: 'Light to light, enter this fire and warm my heart and soul and mind. This I ask and thus I give my weaker light in return.' Blow out your candle and keep it to light for a short period whenever you need light or warmth, naming your need and visualising it coming to fruition as you blow out the candle.

- For a special need for abundance at a time of doubt or dearth, create a ring of golden-coloured coins around a beeswax or pure white candle. Light the candle at dusk and leave it to burn. Replace it at midnight and again at dawn, leaving the final candle to burn through in a safe place. Give the coins to a charity.

- When it has been snowing or the ground is covered with ice or frost, light a small fire in a fireproof dish or an improvised outdoor hearth. On it burn pine cones or needles, or the Sun herbs sage or rosemary. As the snow or ice melts around the fire, throw just a tiny amount of the snow or melting ice on to the fire, not enough to extinguish it, recalling the fusion of ice and fire in the Viking creation myth. As the fire sizzles and smoke rises, hold a stick in the fire so it chars but does not catch light. Brush off the ashes when they are cool and set them in a dish on your altar or in your Crone hearth until dawn. At first light or when you wake, bury them under a living tree. Take the first practical steps to bringing the light and warmth you seek into your life or into a worthwhile cause. Keep the stick near your front door for luck.

Working with Inclement Weather for Transformation

Rather than huddling indoors by the fire in cold or wet weather you can use the energies of the wilder conditions to blow away all the old clutter and irrelevancies in your life.

By melting snow or ice or even a bowl of hailstones in a fireproof dish over a tiny night-light you can also get the energies of transformation and positive change flowing, to be realised in the spring. In Viking lore, hail was called the cosmic seed because it held the potential of new life.

Here I have suggested two basic weather rituals.

A Cleansing Wind Ritual

- On a windy day, find a broken branch or one lying on the ground with a few dead leaves still hanging on it. It is especially potent in a northerly breeze.

- Carry it to a hilltop, keeping it sheltered.

- When you reach the top, stand in the wind and feel all your old problems, situations or negative influences tugging to be free.

- Keep your branch sheltered still and touch each of the leaves, naming a regret, a sorrow, a destructive habit or doubt for each and whispering: 'Go in peace. Leave me, fly free and be restored as healing light.'

- Plant your branch in the earth and walk away. Do not look back. Let the wind do its work. Open your arms wide and run down the hill, free of your burdens.

- Buy a small evergreen plant or find an evergreen bough to set on your altar or in your Crone hearth as a symbol of new growth.

A Snow Ritual for Transformation

- In newly settled snow, make a pathway of footprints, imprinting each slowly and deliberately and making an affirmation of power or assurance concerning future plans or changes for each one. The steps can be related, leading to a goal, or can refer to different changes, either personal or more global.

- Create a possible and realistic time-frame to help you to focus and keep going, for example:

    Step 1. I take in the knowledge that I will complete my media course work by the end of January.

    Step 2. I take in the assurance that I will be offered an interview at my local radio by the spring.

    Step 3. I take in the confidence I will be offered research work by the summer.

    Step 4. I take in the belief that I will be offered my own show by the following New Year.

    Step 5. I take in the certainty that this will be a success and I will be offered a second year's contract.

- Now scoop up snow from the final footprint, saying: 'So do I give substance to my desires.'

- Place the snow in a metal bowl or pan and take it indoors, leaving it to melt naturally while you make practical plans to set the transformation in motion.

- When the snow has melted, plant a pot of bulbs that will flower in spring – daffodils, crocus, hyacinths or other flowers that grow in your region.

- Water the soil with the melted snow, adding a little each day.

- By the time the plant blooms you will, if you have worked to make your dream come true, likewise be blossoming. In the meantime, the budding shoots will be a reminder of what can be achieved.

- If you have no snow, you can make footprints in the earth and scoop up the last one to plant the bulbs in. Melt ice cubes in a bowl, empowering them by moving your hands palm down nine times, the left clockwise and the right anti-clockwise, to balance the energies just above the ice cubes while reciting the steps. You can water the bulbs with the melted ice over a period of days.

Other Ways of Using Winter Weather for Transformation

- Smash thick ice on a pond or in a bucket while chanting: 'I break through all barriers, overcome all obstacles and cut through the prejudice/inertia/injustice/stagnation that obstructs [name the change you seek].' Chant faster and hit the ice harder until you can see the water beneath. With a final 'Ice crack, nought I lack, flow free,' stir the water beneath with your hammer or stick.

- On a rainy day, draw whatever stands in the way of your trans-formation in chalk on paper and leave it in the rain to dissolve.

- Use the power of a thunderstorm as a source of personal energy by leaving a dark fire crystal such as a garnet, iron pyrite (fool's gold), lodestone or jet outside during a thunderstorm. You can then carry your crystal with you as a talisman of sky and fire power on dark, cold days.

- Stand at your altar in any extreme of weather – hail beating on the roof, crashing thunder, high winds or an intense rainstorm. Light a dark red candle and bring the power of the elements down into yourself by focusing on the sound and breathing it slowly but deeply into every fibre of your body. Visualise the rain, the lightning flash or the hail swirling within you so that you are at one with the turbulence outside, and at its height clap your hands over your head and cry: 'We are as one. Power be, with clarity see, make me strong.' Sit quietly and let the sounds recede outside you once more, knowing that you carry within you the courage and strength to make any changes necessary to fulfil your destiny.

Winter is like a storehouse made by our wise ancestors in which we can find all kinds of treasure to illuminate and warm the darkest days of the season or of the soul.

When we stop running from the Crone we may find she is after all our fairy godmother. She may not offer you a pretty dress to go to the ball or a 'happy ever after', but she will give you shelter by her fireside on cold lonely nights and wrap her cloak around you and dry your tears when life has lost its meaning.

6

Dark Angels

Dark Angels are regarded in angelic lore either as those who have become demonic or as those who are fierce and avenging, bringing death and retribution to the unrighteous. But in a universe where darkness is as essential as light and night as day, angels of the night are many and varied, each with their unique positive energies and blessings.

In Appendix III, I have listed angels associated with winter months, with ice and snow, twilight and darkness, planetary bodies and constellations. In this chapter we will be working with seven Archangels, or higher angelic forms, from the gentle Gabriel, Archangel of the moon and dreams, and the shadowy mystical Raziel, to severe Samael, who demands that we revise outworn opinions and shed illusions. Yet all are deeply protective to those who approach them with humility and integrity.

The Dark Angels challenge us to strive for the highest standards in our spiritual and earthly life so that we develop a keen sense of justice and cultivate what is of worth. The process may require that we confront our own shadow side in which may be hidden strong, sometimes negative emotions as well as all kinds of fears that may emerge as night phantoms or terrors. But the experience of these celestial beings is always a positive empowering one, for they are compassionate and will never fail us in the darkest night or coldest day of winter.

Understanding Angels

Angelology, the study of angels, is a very complex, sometimes confusing and contradictory area of knowledge spanning thousands of years and many cultures. Angels are traditionally found in the Judaic, Christian, Islamic and Zoroastrian religions, though other faiths such as Buddhism have their evolved sky beings.

In formal religion angels are regarded as intermediaries between God or the gods and humankind. They are beings of light or spiritual energy who guide humanity and protect the planet. Guardian angels are closest to individuals and so have become the most significant personally. Archangels rank above angels and therefore have less personalised relationships with people, though in magic they usually form the main focus. This is because they represent archetypal or idealised qualities and have the power to offer protection.

Our concept of angels is affected by the society in which we live. However, because angels have been recognised in so many cultures and ages, our view is also influenced by the literature, religious philosophy and art of earlier times. For example, the militaristic qualities of the bands of angels in biblical writings as well as those of Islam or the Jewish esoteric wisdom, the Kabbalah, may stem from the need to defend those faiths against unbelievers and those who still followed earlier Goddess religions or those with many deity forms.

My own favourite depiction of a Dark Angel is the one portrayed by Carlos Schwabe, a painter in late Victorian and early Edwardian times, as a green-winged beautiful woman dressed in jade, surrounded by green light, set against the white snow of a winter cemetery. She is encouraging a frightened man to leave his grave so she may take him to heaven. She has been identified as Azrael, the once fiery Archangel of death.

The real significance of such paintings is that people have expressed angelic energies in many different ways. It can be very helpful to download images of the Dark Angels from the Internet or study them in books. However, it is our own conceptualisation of their energies and the relationship we develop with them that will be of most importance and use to us.

Reassessing the Dark Angels

Though we may visualise angels purely as beings of light and demons as creatures of darkness, some angels and Archangels are specifically called Dark Angels and are usually depicted, especially in older angelic lore and apophycral biblical sources, as divine judges, avenging warriors and harbingers of death or suffering.

However, it may be more appropriate in today's world to think of these powerful beings as cosmic aid workers and spiritual troubleshooters rather than as soldiers or bringers of divine retribution. Their role as judges may also be better understood as evokers of conscience and self-assessment.

Dark Angels also bring protection against the phenomena over which they rule. For example, Suiel, angel of earthquakes, is the special guardian of earthquake zones. A crystal or sachet of herbs blessed in the name of Suiel in a candle ceremony (*see page 120*) can serve as an amulet in the home against the effects of a severe quake.

Dark Angels and Evil

Goodness has quite erroneously become associated with angels of light, and evil with angels of darkness, who have become synonymous with the fallen angels. The fall of Lucifer, or Satan, and his angels was described in the 17th century in John Milton's ten poetic books of *Paradise Lost*. The Old Testament does not refer to Satan, whose name means 'adversary', as a fallen angel, or to the other fallen angels. Indeed, Satan is regarded as an adversary of evil men and is fighting for God. In the Book of Job, he is sent by God to test Job's worthiness. The first reference to the evil Satan comes in the New Testament in Revelation 12:

> [Satan's] tail drew the third part of the stars of heaven [the angels] and cast them to earth and Satan . . . was cast out into the earth and his angels.

It was even later that Jerome and the early Church Fathers developed the concept of the Devil. They associated the Archangel Lucifer, chief angel in heaven, whose name means 'light-bringer', with Satan. By the Middle Ages Satan was accused of refusing to bow down to God's creation, either Adam or Christ, and was identified with the serpent in Eden which brought about Adam's fall.

How could this be? The Church Fathers and later theologians argued that if God were good, he could not have created evil. Conversely, if he were Absolute, no one else could have created it. The only explanation could be that demons must be angels who became too proud/refused to praise God/insisted on keeping their free will rather than surrendering it to God.

Thus, they believed, there was a war in heaven and Lucifer, chief angel and Lord of Light and of the Seraphim, the highest rank of angels, became the Devil. The angels who fought with him were the demons. Those who remained neutral in later lore became the fairies, condemned only to come out at night. The good angels, led by the Archangel Michael, defeated Lucifer and cast him into hell where he was to remain until, according to Revelation, evil would finally be eradicated in the Battle of Armageddon.

Sometimes in different traditions the same angel, for example the Archangel Samael, might be regarded as good or evil, as one of the seven regents of the world, served by two million angels and chief ruler of the fifth heavenly sphere, or as a hideous 12-winged serpent who dragged down the solar system in his fall.

Indeed, in some of the heretical sects of the Church that survived until the Middle Ages, Satan/Lucifer as the former greatest being of light was regarded as taking on the greatest task of all, that of the supreme Dark Angel so that humankind might understand goodness and light in contrast.

Contacting the Dark Archangels

The radiance of the darker Archangel forces comes principally from their association with Fire, though some are also angels of the element Earth. The fire of the dark Archangels is magical alchemical or transforming flame. It flares in the colours of the night – deep emerald, ruby red, midnight blue, amethyst, indigo, silver and burnished gold – and has been a feature of alchemy, of medieval angel magic and of the occult societies of the late 19th and early 20th centuries, which revived the old ways and were greatly influenced by the Kabbalah.

By lighting the candle colour of each of the Archangels (*see pages 113–27*) you can invoke their essential strengths and qualities (rather than the spirit of the angel or Archangel to do your bidding, as was believed by former occultists).

Because fire is such a powerful force in magic, you should only work with your angel fire when you are in a calm, positive frame of mind. To begin psychic exploration when you are angry, jittery or depressed may cause these sensations to be amplified. If you feel like this, spend some time digging a garden, tidying a cupboard or at your night altar stilling your spirit with night breathing or meditation.

With angel fire, always work only with the highest intent and for the greatest good. I have suggested various forms of psychic protection (*see pages 29–34*) or you can draw a crystalline sphere around you (*see page 15*). Since each of the Archangels has special crystals, you could use one of these to breathe in the light of your chosen Archangel.

Incense burning is a traditional method of angel invocation and each of the Dark Archangels has a specific sacred incense *(see pages 113–27)*. You may wish to light extra sticks so that the fragrance is powerful and lifts you above the conscious world.

Method of Making Contact

Magic ancient and modern can sometimes focus exclusively on words and actions that we may fail to harmonise with prevailing energies. It is better to aim at merging with the energies of the focus or ritual than to analyse them or worry about the correct order of words or actions. Angel magic especially is most spiritual and empowering when we allow the divine presence to guide the ritual.

- In your night place, light your angelic candle and incense and hold the angelic crystal between your hands.

- Welcome the angelic presence. Do not always make a petition or request. Instead reflect on the qualities of the Archangel and how they are or could be manifest in your life to help others or the planet.

The Seven Archangels of the Night and Dark Power

Though Archangels, with the exception of Gabriel, are generally viewed as very masculine, they are androgynous and we may perceive them in a compassionate female light in some rituals. Here I have referred to them as 'he' for convenience.

There are any number of Dark Angels/Archangels I could have used, for in later Church literature many angels were regarded as dark or fallen. I have chosen seven who have been invoked in magic and who have, in my view, the most powerful energies of transformation. However, if you want to substitute others, the ideas given here will work with them as well (*see pages 214–18*). Note your rituals and channelling in your Book of Shadows as you explore the different angelic forces.

Azrael/Asrael, the Dark Visionary

Candle colour Deep amethyst

Incense Cedar, juniper or sandalwood

Crystals Obsidian or jet

Known as the angel of death in Hebrew and Christian angelology, he is called Izra'il in Moslem tradition and is one of their four great Archangels.

He is present at the beginning and end of life, writing down in a book the names of people at the time of their birth and erasing them when they die. Some later versions recount that the names of the damned were circled with black.

Azrael brought God the handful of soil from which Adam was created. When a person dies, he severs the soul from the body 40 days after death, staying with each soul on its journey to heaven.

Azrael is also depicted as a giant Archangel spanning with his feet the seventh or uppermost heaven and the bridge between Paradise and hell.

Therefore, though Azrael is awe-inspiring, he is very protective of both the dying and the newborn, setting them on their respective journeys.

Invoke him in times of sorrow, bereavement and all kinds of loss, but also at the beginning of any journey, physical or spiritual, and to protect babies, the very young and old.

Spiritually, you can work with Azrael on issues of mortality and immortality, acknowledging your fears of the finiteness of life and making every day count. He can also help you to sever connections with a way of life that is not fruitful and will show you other realms, especially the past.

Visualise him with a halo of dark purple flames, huge, dark wings and a deep red and purple protective cloak.

An Azrael Ritual for Divination

Dion Fortune, the 20th-century occultist and founder of the esoteric Society of the Inner Light, described working with a divinatory fire known as the fire of Azrael or Asrael. The fire was made of juniper wood, which spits a great deal when lit, cedar and sandalwood, and gave visions of past worlds.

- You can make a fire of any wood, burning dried juniper berries, crumbled sandalwood incense and dried cedar leaves, or adding a few drops of sandalwood and cedarwood essential oils or herbs to the wood before lighting. Alternatively, burn juniper, sandalwood and cedar incense sticks as you kindle the fire. Outdoors you can use incense torches.

- Make your fire on a beach, in a pit of stones and earth, in a flameproof cauldron or a barbecue dish, or build a garden bonfire. If you have a grate indoors, you can light one there. The fire need only be small. If none of these is possible, have a huge purple candle in a cauldron of sand, surrounded by incense sticks.

- Wait till the fire burns low and through half-closed eyes look at the embers and flames. Look especially for any purple flames, as these are Azrael's special form of fire.

- Ask Azrael to show you what will be helpful from the past so that you may understand the present better.

- Allow images to form. The key to successful scrying, whatever medium you are using, is to reprogramme the mind to return to the pictorial way of expressing ideas that you used in childhood. With fire divination you tend to perceive a whole picture rather than separate images.

- Sketch the images you see or write down a very brief description. They are coming from the collective pool of wisdom that we can access when our subconscious minds take charge.

- You can poke the fire between readings to create a new formation.

- You may see visions of past worlds, usually aspects that shed illumination on your current stage of life. They may be actual past lives or symbols of current concerns. They may reveal insights into the world of your actual or spiritual ancestors with whom you have affinity. Whatever the origin, they are usually helpful and may continue in your dreams.

- Finally, thank Azrael for his guidance and ask that you may use the wisdom for the good of others. You may be rewarded by a fleeting image of the Archangel in the flames.

Camael, Camiel or Camiul, Archangel of Courage in Adversity

Candle colour Deep ruby red

Incense Dragon's blood, ginger, mint

Crystals Bloodstone, garnet

According to the sixth-century Syrian monk Dionysus, who created the system of heavenly choirs or ranks, Camael is chief of the angelic order of powers responsible for destroying the demons who threatened to overthrow the world. However, Camael, called Khamael in the Kabbalistic tradition, is also angel of divine love and the patron angel of all who love God.

Camael rules the planet Mars and is a gatekeeper of heaven, guarding souls on their way. He represents divine justice and according to Revelation holds back Leviathan, the evil creature who will consume the souls of sinners on Judgement Day.

Camael is also Archangel of strength and courage and protector of the weak. He strengthened Christ in the Garden of Gethsemane before his crucifixion.

Invoke Camael at times when you need courage or strength because you are vulnerable, to fight injustice or when you need to protect a person, an animal or a place that is under threat. He can also be called on to guard the innocent in war-torn lands.

Spiritually, he will cleanse you of anger and negativity and will help you to overcome your inner dragons.

In magic he is sometimes symbolised by a crouching leopard on a rock, but you can also visualise him as he is often depicted, in a deep red tunic with dark green armour, a halo of dark ruby flames and rich green wings.

A Camael Ritual for Courage in Adversity

Camael rituals tend to act quite quickly and so their purpose can be achieved over a seven-day period (less if a situation is urgent).

- On your night altar after dark, if possible on a Tuesday, Camael's day, set a circle of four deep ruby red candles at the four main compass points. You can focus on any person or place where courage is needed, as well as on your personal empowerment.

- You will need four long pins or thin nails, as iron is the metal of Camael and also represents his mighty sword.

- You will also need ginger or dragon's blood incense, or any other hot spice incense.

- In the centre of the candle circle place a garnet or bloodstone or any other deep red crystal on a red circle of cloth.

- Light the candle in the South first and ask for the aid of Camael, saying: 'I ask as I kindle this flame, mighty Camael, that you cleanse me of any unworthy purpose.' As you speak, press a pin into the candle half an inch from the top on the South-facing surface.

- Light next the candle in the West and say: 'Aid me, mighty Camael, not for vengeance, nor in anger, but that I may have the courage to [name your purpose or challenge].' As you speak, press a second pin in the West surface of the candle.

- Light the candle of the North and say: 'I kindle this flame that you will give me for [name your cause] the strength to persevere, since the way ahead is long and uncertain.' As you speak, press the third pin in the North side of the candle.

- Finally, light the candle in the East, press in the last pin in the

East side of the candle and say: 'I kindle this flame for justice both for me [or whoever is the focus] and by me in this endeavour as I thus call on your name, great Camael.'

• Leave the candles to burn with the pin forming a cross linking the power.

• When the pins fall out, take them and the crystal and wrap them in dark red cloth or paper tied three times with red twine.

• Burn a single dark red candle and a single stick of Camael incense each night for six further nights, at the same time if possible, and place the parcel in front of the candle, repeating aloud the purpose of the ritual and asking Camael for purity of purpose, courage, strength and the integrity to act justly.

• You can extinguish the candle after the ritual, sending strength in Camael's name wherever it is needed, but leave the incense to burn through. Relight the candle each subsequent evening.

• On the seventh night, let the candle burn out. Unwrap the parcel and dispose of the pins and wrappings, but keep the crystal with you, as a talisman of courage should your perseverance fail. Alternatively, leave it on the altar to send power to the endangered person or place.

Cassiel, Archangel of Stillness

Candle colour Indigo/black

Incense Patchouli, thyme, vetivert

Crystals Black onyx, brown jasper

If Camael is the fast-moving Archangel, Cassiel, sometimes called the Archangel of tears and solitude, is the brake on over-intense emotion or rash action. He works on transformation on an inner level. Some have linked him to the primal darkness before creation.

A ruler of the planet Saturn and a prince of the highest seventh heaven, Cassiel stands on the Threshold and weeps for the sins of humankind. He is said to be the Archangel of balance who unifies all things, darkness and light, sorrow and joy, night and day. He is primarily an Archangel of the element Earth.

Invoke Cassiel for patience, for help with all slow-moving

matters and for practical or financial worries that can distract you from the path of spirituality. He is also potent for the conservation of natural resources and traditional values.

Spiritually, Cassiel brings moderation in action, eases addictions, takes away or relieves chronic pain or illness and encourages the development of inner stillness and contemplation.

He is pictured in traditional magic with a beard and riding a dragon. However, you may more easily visualise him swathed in dark robes with indigo flames in his halo and autumnal brown wings.

A Cassiel Ritual to Reduce Chronic Physical or Mental Pain

- Put a small quantity of dried thyme or vetivert in a small open pottery dish.

- Light your indigo candle on your night altar and pass your hands, palms downwards, just above the herbs, the left hand making nine clockwise circles and the right hand nine anti-clockwise circles over the herbs, saying over and over: 'I ask the healing of Cassiel, the silent one, to pass ninefold into these herbs. Blessings be.'

- With both hands, lift the herb dish above the candle and specify the purpose of the ritual: 'I ask you, Archangel who weeps at suffering, to reduce the pain/sorrow of [name the person or animal or yourself]. I seek also patience for what cannot at once be changed, but ask that each day may heal a little more, if it is right to be.'

- Take a small empty plant pot and scoop in a layer of dark soil, saying: 'Thus, Cassiel, do I lay the foundations for restoration. Bless and protect.'

- Add the herbs to the soil, a pinch at a time, saying, 'Pain decrease, sorrow cease. Cassiel, receive into your dark soil and absorb this suffering.'

- When the herbs are gone, cover them with more soil, adding your private invocation and if working on behalf of someone else, visualising them experiencing relief.

- Let the Cassiel candle burn through and then place your plant pot in a dark place for four weeks.

- Bury the soil and herbs under a living tree.

Gabriel, Archangel of the Moon

Candle colour Silver

Incense Jasmine, mimosa, lily

Crystals Moonstone, opal or fluorite

One of the two Archangels mentioned by name in the Old Testament, Gabriel is a wonderful Archangel to work with at night or when you feel alone and afraid.

As Archangel of the Moon and ruler of dreams, Gabriel, whose name means 'God is my strength', is chief Archangel of the night and the alter ego of Michael, the Sun Archangel. Some consider Gabriel a feminine energy.

He is primarily seen as a messenger, his most famous visitation, recorded in the Gospel of St Luke, being to tell Mary that she had been chosen to bear the Son of God. In Islam Gabriel, called Jibril, dictated the Koran to Mohammed.

However, Gabriel is also said to sit on the left hand of God in the seventh heaven, and rules over the first heaven, seated among the clouds and winds, where he commands the angels who take care of the stars.

He is said to be the angel who chooses the souls to be born and cares for them in the womb. He is also an angel of death, but a gentle one, bringing release from sorrow and pain.

Gabriel also rules the West, the element of Water, the tides and rituals to protect water creatures and to cleanse polluted seas, lakes and rivers.

Invoke Gabriel for protection against inclement weather, for travel across water, for taking away sorrow and for diminishing self-destructive tendencies and replacing them with the gentle growth of new hope.

Spiritually, Gabriel the integrator brings increased spiritual awareness and mystical experiences, aids astral travel and significant dreams, and helps us to access unconscious wisdom, especially through prayer and meditation or in a beautiful natural place close to water or the sea.

Visualise Gabriel in silver or clothed in the blue of the night sky with a mantle of stars and a crescent Moon for his halo.

A Gabriel Ritual to Bring Hope to a Dark Night

In Babylonian angelology, Gabriel was the Archangel who brought hope from the Moon, telling despairing people whenever they saw the Moon they should remember his gift. This ritual can bring hope on a dark night, whether a sleepless one or a dark night of the soul. It is also a good fertility rite for any purpose.

Though Gabriel rituals are often performed on the crescent Moon and his special day is Monday, you can focus on him if you wake in the night.

- Go to your night altar and light three silver candles in a triangle, with the single candle at the top.

- Beyond them create a similar triangle of Gabriel incense. Three represents the main Moon phases and also is the number of increase.

- Take a moonstone and place it in half an eggshell or a deep curved silver dish at the centre of the triangle of candles.

- With a silver ink marker pen write on a square of black paper what is in your heart and what you might not even want to tell your best friend, mother or partner. Write it down, no matter how sad, how bad, how unfair you know you are being. Think of it as emptying the negativity you have pressed down in your shadow self that is either spilling over into your dreams and waking world, or weighing you down so you cannot sleep. Once it is gone your shadow will be quite clear and silvery.

- Tear up the paper into tiny pieces, saying as you do so: 'Gabriel, I entrust you with this my burden. Carry it into the night, transform it into moonlight or stardust and leave me free to hope anew.'

- On silver paper, write in black ink what it is you most cherish or desire for the future. Remember this is about you and your inner world, so be totally honest. If, for example, you are desperate for a baby and have shed all the bitterness about people who do not care for their children and yet conceive so easily, ask for that and not for world peace or saving dolphins. Those wishes can come at another time.

- Fold this paper and place it beneath the moonstone in the eggshell or dish at the centre of the candle triangle.

- Ask Gabriel, Archangel of the Moon, messenger to humankind, to send you a sign of blessing.

- Dispose of the remains of the negative message.

- Leave the candles to burn through and sleep with the moonstone and positive message beneath your pillow until the next crescent Moon. During the day shut them in a drawer where they will not be found. You may receive a sign in your dreams.

- On the next crescent Moon turn over the moonstone and message three times, then bury them beneath a Moon tree (*see page 32*) or near water.

Raziel, Archangel of the Hidden World

Candle colour Dark green

Incense Myrrh, pine, poppy

Crystals Aventurine, moss agate

Raziel is called the Archangel of divine mysteries and of secrets, including the secrets of magic. He is credited with writing the esoteric *Book of the Angel Raziel* that contained all earthly and heavenly knowledge. He gave it to Adam as consolation for losing Eden, but other angels became jealous and threw it into the sea. God ordered Rahab, angel of the deep caverns of the sea, to restore it to Adam. Thereafter the book passed to Enoch, then to Noah and finally to King Solomon, who derived from it his own magical powers and wisdom. It is this mystical knowledge that has inspired occult magicians through the ages right up to the present day. However, only Raziel can reveal its deepest secrets to those angels and mortals he favours.

Raziel is also the angel of the unknown and unknowable because he stands at the veil that separates God from all creation. He is one of the Cherubim. These are not at all like the chubby winged babies of Victorian paintings but are wise sphinx-like creatures who guard the hidden knowledge of God.

Invoke Raziel for psychic and mystical knowledge and to help you access your own deep unconscious wisdom, discover past lives and develop your own prophetic voice. Call on him too if you are confused, need to discover a secret or suspect that others are deceiving you.

Spiritually, allow him to communicate with your shadow self and so guide you to bring out your hidden potential and to overcome your fears about your own inadequacies.

Raziel is a shadowy Archangel whom you may contact most easily at twilight, on misty days and before dawn, but may not see clearly. Visualise him in grey swirling robes like an ever-changing grey-green sea with deep green flares in his halo or as an outline behind a dark grey semi-transparent curtain.

A Raziel Ritual for Working with Your Shadow

- Just after dusk, light a tall grey or deep green candle so that it is directly reflected in a large mirror.

- Sit so that the candle flame is level with your eyes and in front of you so that your face is half in shadow.

- Experiment with moving your face slowly so that you merge with the pattern of light and shadow.

- Visualise the protective veiled form of Raziel behind you.

- Say: 'Raziel, who knows all secrets, all mysteries, reveal to me the hidden parts of my true self I fear yet need to bring into the light.'

- If you look through half-closed eyes you may not see any direct images in the mirror, but the patterns of flickering light on the reflective surface may trigger internal images. Do not be afraid, for there are no monsters within. Indeed, we are all far less terrible than we imagine ourselves to be.

- As you gaze into the mirror, you may see a child, your inner child. This child may seem sad because they never come out to play, or they may be smiling, reminding you of all those childhood dreams you have yet to fulfil.

- Finally, say to Raziel, if you want to: 'Wise Archangel who stands at the veil between present and future, lift it if it is right for me to glimpse the possibilities that lie before me.' You will not see death or disaster, for the future is not fixed. What you will see is a number of pathways, each leading to different goals which may be represented symbolically and which you can now assess.

- Look directly into the mirror once more and thank Raziel for his wisdom and blessings.

- Blow out the candle and spend the rest of the evening in practical activity to put into motion one of your future goals. Write up any future life images and make a resolution to let your inner child out to play and inspire you at least once a week.

This ritual should not be carried out more than once every six months unless you come to a major point of change.

Samael/Sammael, Angel of Severity and Personal Integrity

Candle colour Deep blue

Incense Fennel, basil, sage

Crystals Lapis lazuli, sodalite

Like Camael, Samael is associated with the planet Mars and if you wish, you can adopt the colours, incenses and crystals of Camael (*see page 115*).

Samael is sometimes called the Severity of God and as such is an angel of cleansing fire and of righteous anger. He is said to be one of the seven regents of the world and to be served by two million angels, and also to be the Dark Angel who in the guise of the serpent tempted Eve and fathered the children of Lilith, first wife of Adam.

This demonisation of Samael appeared in *The Alphabet of Ben Sira*, written between the sixth and eleventh centuries. The demonic pairing of Lilith and the fallen Samael is especially interesting, if inaccurate, since more modern feminist secular versions make Lilith a form of the ancient Earth Mother whose worship was defeated by the worshippers of the sky god Yahweh. Samael may have been an ancient earth god who later became associated with the fallen angels and sometimes even Satan.

Rather than being afraid of this evil reputation projected on to Samael, we should regard him as a true tester of faith and someone who introduced the concept of free will into the Garden of Eden.

Samael may not be an easy angel to work with and you might like to leave him until later in your explorations. He does challenge the status quo and demands that we examine our motives and make our own choices, rather than go along with the majority view or the way things have always been. He demands integrity and honesty of purpose and so we may have to do a fair amount of cleansing of the dark corners where we keep our personal prejudices and excuses for inertia.

Invoke Samael for all matters where truth is of the essence, for making your own decisions and if necessary standing alone for an unpopular cause you believe is right. Call on him also in rituals to relieve the suffering of oppressed minorities and endangered species.

Spiritually, use his energies for shaking off inertia, for challenging yourself to high standards in every aspect of your life and for rethinking ideas and beliefs you may have clung to for years but which may need revising. He is a good angel to invoke before dawn or towards the end of winter when you can feel the sap rising spiritually.

Visualise him in midnight blue and red, with blue and red flames in his halo and midnight blue wings, sweeping through the skies waking the slumbering angels and scattering slumbering mortals on Earth.

A Samael Ritual for Cleansing Fear and Prejudice

- In the centre of your night altar place your silver or crystal bowl and surround it with a circle of three dark red and two midnight blue candles. Five is the number of change.

- Burn one of your Samael incenses.

- Light the candle at the North of the bowl and say: 'Mighty Samael, I ask you cleanse me of [a prejudice, an area of stagnation or inertia to making desired change].'

- Continue naming areas of stagnation in your life until you have lit all your candles. You can also focus on more global prejudice or bigotry.

- Gaze into the centre of the bowl, concentrating on a circle of light, and visualise Samael at the centre.

- Take a red and a blue candle in your hands, drip the wax on to the surface of the water and as it swirls, name an image that you may see in the coloured wax or in your mind. Continue to drop more wax until you have a second and third image. The moving images will highlight the areas where change can be made and once the wax has set it will evoke a picture of how this may be achieved.

Uriel, Archangel of Alchemy and Transformation

Candle colour Burnished gold

Incense Frankincense, bay and copal

Crystals Rutilated quartz, tiger's eye

Uriel, whose name means 'fire of God', is the most dazzling of the angels of the night. Though he is called regent of the Sun, this is the dark Sun, the Sun at midnight, the eye of the universe, a magical concept of seeing the archetypal spiritual fire at the darkest hour.

Uriel is the Archangel who brought alchemy to humankind. Alchemy is the sacred art of transmuting base metal into gold by reducing it to the primal black matter and then, by chemico-magical processes, striving to extract and refine spiritual as well as actual gold, the key to finding the way back to Paradise. Uriel also instructed Moses in the Kabbalah, the esoteric system of Hebrew spirituality and magic by which humankind can also be reunited with God.

Until we are ready to return by our own efforts, though, Uriel guards the gates of the Garden of Eden with his fiery sword. The salvation that he offers is the kind whereby we use the wisdom we are given to find our own path to enlightenment.

Uriel is said to be the brightest Archangel, a pure pillar of fire, and so can best be invoked just before dawn to mark the transition to a day when we need to make significant efforts. He also blazes in a fiery sunset. As an angel of the North and the element Earth, he can bring warmth to the winter and melt the snows with his flaming sword.

Invoke Uriel for protection, for change of all kinds, for the fulfilment of a long-term spiritual path, for quelling anger in others and transforming our own fury, jealousy, resentment and spite into the impetus for positive change, and for focusing single-mindedly on making the world a better and safer place.

Spiritually, Uriel will inspire us to work with angels, Devas and higher spiritual essences, to perfect our vision of divine realms and to refine our spiritual nature by burning away our deep-seated desire for comfort and partial vision.

Visualise him in rich burnished gold and ruby red with the brightest flame-like halo of all the Dark Angels, like a bonfire blazing in the darkness, and a fiery sword.

A Uriel Ritual to See the Sun at Midnight

Becoming aware of what is said to be the greatest power of the night, the dark Sun at midnight, has always been an important step in spiritual work. It is like a full solar eclipse with fire rays leaping from behind a pure black disc in a darkened sky. Some people have explained the experience as like cutting a hole through the centre of the world and if you are in London at midnight seeing the Sun shining in Australia at noon. Certainly it is a powerful visualisation exercise that will prepare you for any spiritual challenge.

• Because this is quite an advanced spiritual process, begin by imagining fire rays behind a black disc in a pure black midnight sky. At first the process will be entirely an internal one, although if you do work looking at actual darkness the imagining processes will begin to mingle with the external scene as you practise this visualisation a number of times. In time, with Uriel's help, you will find that the process happens at peak moments when you are standing looking out at the darkness.

• Light a gold candle on your altar and one of Uriel's incenses.

• Stand in front of the altar looking through the light at the night sky. If you cannot face a window from this position, set a table with a dark cloth where you can see the sky. A window does provide a frame for the dark Sun image. Alternatively work outdoors where there are no street lights.

• Continue to visualise the shining black disc in the centre of the darkness, more iridescent than the rest of the sky.

• Say: 'Uriel, Dark Angel, Regent of the Dark Sun, let me see the spiritual gold of alchemy, that I too may transform my life.'

• Look into the candle through half-closed eyes, especially the halo of light around the flame. You are going to project this into the sky around your black disc.

- Say: 'Uriel, Power of Dark Fire, take this golden fire and make the Sun blaze in the blackness, bringing day even in the midst of night, uniting all experience.'

- Draw the light of the candle into your fingertips by passing your hands, palms down, nine times above and to each side of the flame, moving your left clockwise and your right anti-clockwise in unison. Be very careful not to hold your hands too near the flame and make sure you are not wearing trailing sleeves.

- Visualise your fingertips and hands sparkling with the radiance.

- Now thrust your fingers diagonally forwards towards the black disc you are visualising in the midnight sky, saying as you do so: 'Uriel, flame fly, ignite the darkness that there may be light.' Direct the last word to the skies.

- Close your eyes, open them, blink and you may be rewarded by shooting flames or sparks around the black Sun disc.

- If not, imagine it and with perseverance you will bring the opposites together, dark and light, and create your own very tiny but significant alchemical miracle.

In time you will be able to see the Sun at midnight for longer. This is a good ritual for when you know that your survival, in whatever area of your life, is under threat and you must fight in the morning.

As you work with Dark Angels, you may find that you become increasingly aware of angelic presences in your life, not only at night but also at twilight or on dark winter days.

In my own case it was a statue of an angel that inspired me to hope. I was sitting despondently in the low winter sunshine in a dark recess in Amiens cathedral in northern France last November. I was troubled because my older daughter had been treated very badly by her former employers and like any mother I was carrying her hurt and anxiety in my heart.

I looked up and in front of me was a statue of a weeping angel. He was a tiny child with wings on a high marble tomb, crying for the sorrows of humanity. I had walked past the statue earlier, dismissing it as sentimental, though it was one of the treasures of the cathedral. Now the angel was suffused in tiny dancing rainbows, which also stained the white columns, so that I was sitting within a moving rainbow. The colours reflected on my hands and moved as I moved. Suddenly I was filled with certainty, not that there would be any easy solution for my daughter, for we were facing an international company set to crush a 20-year-old, but that all would be well in the end.

I have an image of my rainbow angel on my computer and though six months later we are still fighting for justice for my daughter and money is running out, my rainbow angel still gives me strength and assurance that all will be well.

7

Dreams and Astral Travel

The worlds of dreams and astral travel are interlinked and in a number of cultures and ages have been regarded as no less important than daytime physical journeying. Among people as far apart as Greenland and New Guinea the soul is believed to travel astrally during sleep to a special dream world. These experiences are used on waking to guide decisions.

The ancient Greeks likewise considered that the soul left the body during sleep. Even recognisable characters in a dream were considered to be deities in disguise bringing messages. Hippocrates, the Greek founder of modern medicine, believed that in sleep the soul could see in image form the causes and cures of illness.

In modern times, the greatest influence on dream interpretation has been the psychiatrist and philosopher Carl Gustav Jung. He combined ancient dream lore with Freud's beliefs that dreams expressed material from the unconscious mind that was repressed during the daytime. Jung accepted that recurring dreams drew attention to important issues we ignore in the daytime. However, he also believed that through dream symbols we could understand and heal our own unrecognised conflicts and questions about birth, death, control, letting go, past, present and future, immortality and even magic, which he considered an important untapped power within the human psyche.

Spontaneous dreams are the most significant revelation of night wisdom. They can alert us to new opportunities and creative solutions and even warn us about future events. This is possible because in sleep we do not have in place our conscious blocks that keep us firmly within the parameters of the immediate. Inventions have been discovered in dreams and contact made with angels and with beloved deceased relations (*see also pages 179–80*).

In this chapter we will use the world of dreams as a way of accessing information not available to our daytime mind, learn to control our dreams so that we can use them as a source of personal power and learn to travel in sleep, like the ancients, to other realms.

Working with Dreams

Of course not all dreams are psychic. Some are part of the process of sorting and discarding mental clutter from the day. But even these are worth recalling and cataloguing so you can tune in to your inner feelings. You may uncover priorities and deep-seated needs that have become buried beneath the demands of everyday life.

However, some vivid dreams transport us to an unfamiliar place or time where we may seem to spend hours or even days. We may be part of a family or community that seems as real as our daytime home and we may return on subsequent nights.

On the dream plane we may also enter into meaningful dialogues with people from our past who may either have died or left our sphere. We may also talk to significant people in our present lives. Some may report a similar dream on the same night. Wise men and women, kings, queens or famous leaders may offer advice or give us information that is subsequently proved true. On waking there may be a tremendous sense of loss.

You can increase your chances of dreaming creatively by relaxing before bed, perhaps taking a walk in the darkness or spending a few minutes in the garden or on your balcony if you feel enervated. Have a bath in soothing oils such as rose, chamomile or lavender, and listen to gentle music before you sleep. There are some excellent tapes available. I find Buddhists' chants slow a whirling mind.

Years ago people said their prayers before they went to sleep and asked for protection during the night. Rather than a formal invocation, formulate a few words of thanks and ask for your

personal deity, angel or the benign force of the night to stand
sentinel while you sleep.

Recalling Your Dreams

The most crucial factor for dream interpretation is to recall the
dream. Within a few minutes of waking, details may fade. Memory
tidies up the experience and even the wisdom or knowledge we
acquired becomes clouded. However, recall of dreams increases
dramatically the more we practise.

- Keep a notebook and pen at your bedside or, if you prefer, a tape
  recorder. Whenever you wake from a dream or even a nightmare,
  switch on the light and write down the details, characters,
  feelings, dialogue and a number of key words to help you recall
  the overall impressions when you analyse the dream material
  later.

- If you wish to return to the dream, visualise one of the last or the
  strongest pleasurable images or scenes and draw it closer in your
  mind until you are enfolded within it.

- If you do not want to go back into the dream, picture yourself
  floating on pink fluffy clouds through a starlit sky or enclosed in
  a warm dark blanket, gently rocking in the cosmic cradle. This is
  also a good way of overcoming insomnia.

Analysing Your Dreams

Once you have recalled your dream, the next step is to analyse its
meaning.

- In the evening, after dark, sit quietly in front of your night altar
  and light a dusky pink or purple candle, and have a small soft
  light by which to read your notes.

- Reread the dream material aloud or listen to the dream tape.

- Now softly tell yourself the story of the dream, if you wish
  adding details that you did not recall but which seem to fit.

- As you talk you may relive the feelings and impressions. If you
  do not force connections, you will intuitively understand where

the dream fits into your everyday world and perhaps the new directions in which your psyche is progressing.

• If an image puzzles you, draw it in a circle and add spokes radiating as if from a wheel. At the end of each spoke write down a word or phrase that spontaneously emerges in your mind, or perhaps a related image.

• Circle any of these new words that seem significant and draw spokes from them until you have an interconnected web.

• Record details of the dream and the insights gained at your night altar in a special section in your Book of Shadows.

• Start an A–Z list on your computer or in a notebook and in time you will create your personalised dream dictionary (*see also Appendix I*).

Incubating Your Dreams

Throughout history people have induced dreams to answer specific questions. The first recorded 'dream incubation' was practised by the ancient Egyptians, who used candles or lamps to induce creative dreams in the third century BC.

In this tradition, called *dreaming true,* someone with a question went to a cave that faced South and sat in the darkness gazing at a candle flame until they saw in it the face or form of a deity. They would then sleep in the cave and in dreams the guardian god or goddess would bring the answer to the problem.

I discovered a more sophisticated version of this in the British Museum in London. An Egyptian text from Thebes, dated around AD 200, of the period known as the Roman kingdom, described how the would-be dreamer burned frankincense in front of a lighted lamp and wrote a question around the rim of the lamp. Then they gazed into the lamplight until they saw the image of a deity in the halo of the lamp. They could not speak to anyone but had to walk into a red mist as sleep came on. The deity would emerge from the mist to bring the answer on the dream plane.

The Egyptians also created special dream temples in honour of Serapis, god of sleep. Seekers would carry out rituals of cleansing and prayer before going to sleep in the Serapeum where Serapis would send a dream. Dream interpreters could be consulted in the temple if the meaning was not clear.

- Use either your bedroom or soft cushions in your night place.

- Wait until you are sleepy and it is very dark.

- Light a stick of frankincense and a large white candle and sit with your eyes half-closed, gazing into the flame.

- Breathe slowly and deeply and visualise the candle flame expanding into a huge white sphere.

- As you do so, allow a question or a few words summarising an important issue in your life to run though your mind like a gentle mantra. Visualise the letters flowing in spirals around the candle like smoke.

- As you gaze into the expanding candle flame, you may see a figure or one may appear in your mind. Allow them to take shape spontaneously. You may recognise your night guardian, an angel or a wise man or woman, a Chinese sage, a monk, nun, a Druid, Druidess or a true Romany. Some people believe that what we see at such moments of stillness is our higher evolved self, the part of our soul that connects us with the realms of spirit.

- Once you have identified your figure, blow out the candle, asking silently that the wisdom they have to impart may come to you while you sleep.

- Lie quietly and recite once more your question, visualising the words floating away like wisps of smoke against the night sky.

- Then go to bed.

- When you wake, make a note of any vivid symbols you saw in your dreams, for they will hold the key to your question, even if you do not recall your guardian appearing in the dream.

- The next evening, go to your night altar and light another stick of frankincense and two or three white candles so you have sufficient light to read by.

- Write down what each symbol suggests to you, without trying to rationalise what it ought to mean. If in doubt, weave a story around them to provide an outcome. Add them to your dream dictionary.

Using the Healing Power of Dreams

A similar idea was practised in ancient Greece, where dream temples were dedicated to Aesculapius or Aesclepios, the Greek deity of healing, who was taught his arts by the centaur Chiron (*see page 73*). They were dedicated to evoking dreams that brought healing or which suggested a cure to those who slept within the temple.

Sophocles built the first shrine dedicated to Aesculapius in Athens in the fifth century BC. Other shrines followed in rapid succession, the most famous being at Epidaurus, which became a major healing centre. Over 300 active Aesculapian healing temples still existed throughout Greece and the Roman Empire in the second century AD.

People seeking a cure would carry out purifying rituals in the external chambers until they were given signs that the time was right to enter the inner sleep temple to be healed. Animal sacrifices were made and the dreamer would sleep on the skin of the sacrificed animal, which was usually a ram.

Aesculapius or his daughters Panacea and Hygea would visit the sick in a dream and either touch a wound or painful area and cure it or suggest remedies for the illness. Priests or priestesses would help to interpret the dream and in later times would have herbs, potions and ointments so the dreamer could follow the instructions given in the dream immediately. Many of the temples were built close to healing waters.

How could this work? American neo-Freudian psychoanalyst Karen Horney believed that dreams expressed a level of the true self that was not available during waking consciousness and so could express accurate information about the psyche and personality. Thus in sleep we can access knowledge of the causes of illness and the treatment that will help. According to Jung, we tap into the collective well of universal wisdom to obtain information. Our self-healing system is also activated by the dream.

If you are exhausted or unwell, but there is no obvious cause and the illness does not warrant urgent medical intervention, you can ask God/the Goddess/a healing Archangel such as Cassiel or your higher self to send healing while you are asleep.

- Before you go to bed, have a bath, adding a few drops of a gentle healing essential oil such as chamomile, rose or lavender.

- In your bedroom or using cushions in your night place, at a safe distance light a natural beeswax candle as a focus for healing.

- Light a sandalwood or myrrh incense stick.

- If possible, sleep on a sheepskin or furry rug or blanket, which can be made of a synthetic fibre if you do not wish to use animal skin.

- Sit so you are facing the candle and in its flame visualise the face of a wise healer. Allow the form of the healing essence to build up quite spontaneously in the candle.

- Speaking to the healer, list each symptom or area of pain or your state of mind and let any related worries flow quite naturally. You can also use this method to ask for healing for someone you love or a family pet.

- If you wish, you can place the candle on a heatproof tray and on a long thin strip of white paper write down key words to represent the symptoms.

- When you have finished, consign the paper to the flame and let it burn away naturally on the tray. Or you can burn dark threads for each problem area as you name them aloud.

- You can bury the collected ash in the morning beneath a living tree.

- As you blow out the candle, see the illness crumbling into tiny black dots, which are absorbed by the light as it flows into the cosmos.

- Close your eyes and float on fluffy white clouds.

Understanding the Messages

Your dream may be couched in symbols which may reveal the underlying situation that caused the illness and its resolution. But dreams are frequently remarkably explicit and easy to interpret.

For example, if you have a skin irritation and you dream of being immersed in a bed of soft rose petals, it might indicate rose oil could be helpful. You might dream of a certain food turning black and tasting bitter or mouldy as you bite into it, which could represent a particular food allergy. On the other hand, you might dream of a remote holiday island and diving into a clear pool beneath a cascading waterfall. This would indicate that the skin irritation was caused by stress, emotional as well as physical. Drinking or swimming in pure water would detoxify your system and a holiday would clear up your stressed skin and psyche.

You may also notice that after a dream the condition improves. This can occur whether the dream is spontaneous or induced by the method I suggested above. In some way your natural immune system has been activated by direction on this psychic level.

- If the dream meaning is not clear, draw a series of boxes in a grid formation and write down each symbol in its own box.

- Hold a pointed amethyst or smoky quartz, your wand or a pendulum in your power hand (the one you write with) over each symbol in turn and ask the crystal to indicate which is the most relevant factor. You will feel a tugging downwards or the pendulum will feel heavy over the correct symbol.

- As with conventional dream symbols, draw a circle around the symbol your pendulum identified and write as many associations as come spontaneously.

- You can ask the pendulum to continue making choices until the meaning is clear.

Creating a Lucid Dream State

The next important stage is to become aware when you are in a dream so that you can manipulate the action and change the ending. In this way you can rehearse potential opportunities or confrontations with which you find it difficult to cope in everyday life. Once you are in control and not just a passive actor, you can also turn bad dreams into good ones, banishing demons, fighting monsters, winning through obstacles and expressing feelings you find hard to acknowledge in your waking life.

This state, called *lucid dreaming*, releases a great deal of suppressed psychic power and enables you to work in harmony with your shadow or night self. Once you direct the play you can transform all kinds of taboo material locked within you without fear of being overwhelmed or spooked by your own inner demons.

How is this possible? If you are aware you are dreaming you know also that you are in no danger and you can control the monsters, fly, swim or float out of danger, create success scenarios and carry the power and confidence back into your waking world.

What is more, research suggests that accelerated physical healing occurs after a period of creative lucid dreaming, perhaps because on a psychic level you take control and, as in the ancient dream temples, you spontaneously trigger your self-healing mechanisms. You are creating your recovery through your dreams.

Most people do have a spontaneous lucid dream at some time, and as you work with dream incubation and healing this faculty may develop quite naturally.

- Once more you can work either in your night place or your bedroom.

- This time burn light sleep-inducing incense such as musk or jasmine and only use a very enclosed small night-light in a safe place that cannot be knocked over.

- Lie in the dimness and visualise yourself in a happy dream that has just a few main images. Emotion is a good way of triggering psychic senses.

- Run through the dream in your mind, expanding every feeling as you walk through the dreamscape. It may be easier to use a fairy tale or rich historical story in which you take the starring role, but avoid high drama or conflict at this stage.

- Near the beginning of the dream story, insert a dream sign, something you would not see in the everyday world – a talking animal or bird, a rainbow-coloured flower or a gigantic butterfly.

- Say out loud: 'When this [symbol] appears I know I am dreaming.' Continue with the scenario.

- Evoke the symbol two or three times in your fantasy, repeating each time: 'When the [symbol] appears, I will know that I am dreaming.'

- Let yourself fall asleep, holding the dream symbol in your thoughts as you walk into a dream.

• This technique may not work the first time round, although you may experience a particularly vivid dream and a fleeting awareness that you are dreaming. Repeat the same dream visualisation, symbol and words each night before sleep until you make the transition to the dream plane.

• Once you are aware of being in a dream you can climb in seconds to the top of a high mountain, dive into water and swim, float or fly through the air, while knowing you can return at any time. You can direct your dream.

• Write down the outcome and any special symbols in your Book of Shadows.

Once you are used to lucid dreaming techniques you can use your awareness of being in a dreamscape to travel to different lands, actual and mythical, and to other times. You can experience the baking heat of Egypt and watch a procession to celebrate the rising of Sothis the Dog star or climb up dark staircases in 16th-century Europe to study ancient books in an alchemist's laboratory. The choice is yours.

Astral Travel

As I mentioned at the beginning of this chapter, people in a number of cultures believe that in sleep we project our minds or our inner spirit bodies to travel astrally to other realms. You can also begin to do this when you are awake.

By initially visualising yourself in a scene, you can direct your astral journeys to specific places and times. Once you begin working with thought forms, memories, ideas, myths and legends, you are no longer restricted by material reality. You can travel psychically not only to actual places and historical events but also to those lands created by the imagination of ancient myth-weavers or religious visionaries. Indeed, the visions we have of angelic realms were often first seen by astral travellers in an earlier age and confirmed by subsequent mind voyagers who linked into and added to the power and beauty of the original vision.

Once created, these thought worlds do not cease to exist, but are passed down the generations through ancient stories and poems. The imaginary realms become a memory bank, a psychic World

Wide Web that you can access once you tune in. If you are bound by the demands of the logical world, read a book of fairy tales or watch fantasy movies to reawaken your imagination.

Your First Waking Astral Journey

Since astral means 'of the stars', our first astral journey while we are awake can be to those constellations, stars and planets whose energies we invoked in our earlier work.

When you visit these starry places, you are not seeing the hard rock or the molten gases, but the essential energies of the celestial body. Its aura or psychic energy field is translated by the interaction between it and our own aura into a symbolic waking dreamscape that can teach and empower us.

The following is an extension of our earlier visualisation work (*see pages 64–5*). The crucial difference is that you are actually projecting your mind or spirit body on to the planet or star and can go wherever you wish, even hopping from star to star or constellation to constellation and visiting some of those like Sirius B that can only be seen through a telescope.

- Before your astral journey, visualise your night crystalline protection around you (*see pages 15–16*) or use one of the protective methods (*see pages 30–2*). You are sensitive psychically while inducing astral travel and do not wish to exhaust yourself.

- On a clear night, focus on a constellation, star or planet that you can see and with which you feel an affinity. You may find it easiest to lie on a camp bed or blanket so that you can look directly upwards.

- Mark a pathway through other stars by which you will travel and as you gently inhale and exhale, draw yourself up, as though climbing a tree of stars, until when you reach the top you float or fly slowly in your mind's vision to your chosen destination.

- Focus on the guardian of your chosen sphere and see them framed in a doorway of light. Go through the doorway and allow the scene to unfold. (If you found your star visualisation work difficult, create further doorways and archways and look through each to find the best direction in which to travel.)

• When you feel the focus fading, relax into the gentle floating sensation and you will notice that the sphere is receding. Call goodbye and thanks to your star guardian host or hostess and float gently to Earth once more.

Once in space, the galaxies are yours to explore. On each astral journey you can travel to yet undiscovered planets and star systems. You may meet travellers from different worlds as well as the inhabitants of other worlds, strange animals, godlike peoples, even angelic beings. Some may talk to you or show you places you need to visit.

Remember nothing can harm you, especially if you begin your space travel from a star whose guardian you know. Your spirit body is still part of your physical body. You have just moved into another mode of operating. Just as when you are driving a car and looking at the scenery, in an emergency your mind will instantly switch to conscious mode and you can return to the everyday world at any time. However, a gentler transition is easier on your psyche and is generally spontaneous.

Keep notes in your Book of Shadows of the places you visit and any messages you bring back and in time you will have a whole galactic web.

Astral Travel from Your Night Place

Some people hate the idea of floating above their bodies and of course that is just one way we visualise travelling in our minds or our spirit bodies. You do not need to travel upwards if you adopt the following technique. It is also good if you wish to visit a specific place or time.

Remember to abide by the usual rules of hospitality. Do not enter a home unless invited by the spirit host or hostess and do not attempt to change any events. Since it is all thought work, you cannot come to harm and can move on or return to your night place by counting down from ten to nought at any time.

If you are disturbed during your journey you will not be lost in time, but will return instantly to reality, sorting out a family crisis or answering the mobile phone you forgot to put on silent mode.

• Wait until after dusk and light an indigo or deep purple candle.

- Burn sage or sandalwood incense. These are especially potent for astral work.

- Focus on a symbol of the time and place you wish to visit – a picture, a statue or an artefact. You can use reproductions. Working with the Tarot card scenes of a highly illustrated pack such as the Rider Waite or Morgan Greer is also a good stimulus. Tarot cards can offer many entry points into other dimensions through waterfalls or castle doorways, or by following streams or entering forests.

- When you are ready, place your symbol on the night altar in front of the candle. Hold your large dark crystal with candlelight reflecting on it and visualise a doorway of light in it.

- See the doorway increasing in size and brilliance until you are standing in front of it and it swings open inwards.

- At first you may wish just to look through the doorway on to the scene, but when you are ready you can enter. You will see your night guardian just inside, acting as guide and protector.

- Count from one to ten slowly and take ten steps forwards in your vision into the astral world.

- If, in your mind's eye, you stand still and look all around, you will see your symbol or the scene you studied. Move through this, observing carefully everything around you down to the last detail – colours, sounds and fragrances. Watch wizards, Druids or priestesses at work or in worship. Walk through temples and shrines, and perhaps witness ceremonies at stone circles or the first farmers invoking the deities of the harvest.

- You may find that after a few astral experiences you can interact with some of the people you meet. Restrict yourself to two or three questions on each visit. You can return to the same world a number of times or explore different vistas.

- The experience will end in its own time. Though you may feel you have been away for days, in fact only a few minutes will have elapsed. You will become aware of the door and beyond it the crystal, and your guardian will return you to the entrance.

- Count from ten to one slowly, reach the door and pass through.

• Sit quietly in the candlelight, drifting in and out of the other world until it is quite separate and then fades.

You can use other scenarios, such as moving through a crystalline tunnel leading from your night crystal towards a point of light. You might visualise a river flowing on the other side of the crystalline doorway and travel by boat.

Shamanic Dream Work

Shamans are the magician priest and priestess healers in indigenous communities around the world. They are found in India, Australia, Japan and China, Siberia and Mongolia, Africa, North, Central and South America, and among the Bedouins of the Middle East.

Shamans, who can be of either sex, are expert astral travellers, riding their night steeds through the skies. They may also travel down tunnels deep into the Earth or climb the world tree towards the Pole Star (sometimes working with an actual tree). Their spirit bodies may ascend on the smoke curling upwards from a central fire through a hole in the top of a yurt or large tent of skins, or they may dive deep into the dark ocean by focusing on a pot of darkened water. Theirs is said to be the oldest religion in the world and shamanic visions of other worlds may have given rise to later more formal religious images of heaven and hell. Shamans work primarily at night by the light of a single lantern or a fire, which forms the focal point of many ceremonies.

In the Amazon regions and in Africa some spirit masks worn by shamans are so sacred that that they may only be viewed in the dark. The Amazonian shaman sits on a special stool, carved with powerful predator animals and birds of prey. It is believed the shaman can contact spirit doubles of these creatures through the carvings. There is a place in the middle of the stool where the elder or shaman establishes connection with the spirit world and sometimes merges with or rides on the back of the spirit creature.

Among the Tukano of the Amazon basin shamans would wear necklaces of jaguar teeth to signal their capacity to change into their feline alter ego so they might travel through the night. As these spirit creatures they would journey to the upper spirit realms of the wise ancestors or to the lower realms of magical animals, jungles and deep rivers, where the mistress of the animals or fishes waited to release the herds into the world for hunting.

By adopting the practices of shamanism in dream work, we can move up a notch or two in psychic awareness and enter the world of mythology as though it were a physical plane in order to obtain power and healing.

Drumming, dancing, chanting and shaking rattles all play a vital role in helping the shaman to attain a higher state of consciousness. You can experiment with drumming or dancing to drum music and see if this method works well for you. However, we will work primarily with the silence of the night.

The Silence of the Night

- You can work in the open air in a dark place or at your night altar. Wait until you are sleepy. If your mind is not stilled, use night breathing to create a dark circle of calm within you, like the external tent of skins.

- Light a single large incense stick in the centre of your altar or in front of you in a safe container.

- Light tiny night-lights, again in fireproof containers, or switch on three or four small battery torches.

- Focus on any sounds you can hear, whether urban or country, in your mind's ear turning down the volume so that they fade. Visualise a thick mist coming down, muffling them.

- Extinguish one of your lights and in your mind move back into the stillness within.

- Continue, moving deeper into your inner mind sanctuary, until all the lights are gone and there is only the curl of smoke from the incense.

- Swaying very slightly, ascend the smoke and then spiral down again, up and down continuously until you become the smoke and can rise in your mind as the smoke.

- Let the smoke rise up, passing through an imaginary opening in the ceiling if you are working indoors. Merge with the darkness and be still so you too are perfectly motionless in the heart of silence and darkness.

- Remain there totally at one with the first night before creation until you find yourself separating out again, becoming the swirling smoke and then yourself observing the smoke.

- Light a single night-light or torch and as you look into the light you can travel to magical places, realms of talking animals, lands made of shimmering crystal . . . You can dive with the rainbow fish, soar like the eagle of the night, swoop bat-like in front of the Moon.

- Wherever you travel, you will find little crystals shining in moonlight or starlight. They are parts of your essential self that have become detached or that you have given away out of love or fear, perhaps over many years. Now you can gather them up and reclaim them, make yourself whole and connected again like the small child with a universe to explore. It will take many months of such journeys – perhaps you will only travel once a month or less. But over time you will regain a sense of integration and this may be one of the greatest gifts of night magic.

Experiment also gazing deep into darkened water, which can represent a dark hole into the depths of the sea. Hold the carving or statue of a predatory jungle animal or bird and rise up though the silence of the jungle or over the trees to other worlds.

Once dreams assume real significance in our lives we suddenly find our horizons are wider and that sleep can be as empowering and often more exciting than the daytime world.

8

Dark Places in Nature

I stood in the shadows of one of the inner caves at Wookey Hole; the famous caverns in the west of England. The rest of the party had gone ahead with the guide to walk across the narrow bridge over the deep green river flowing through the high-vaulted earth rainbow of coloured rocks. I wanted to be alone just for a few moments in the shadows of this cavern close to the impenetrable water, in the place once dubbed the Witch's Skullery because of the human remains that had been washed here as the river levels rose.

The tales of Wookey were lurid, like many of those associated with caves over the millennia. Medieval clergy feared the wraiths and night demons that they believed served the witch who practised her arts in the cave, away from the eye of the Sun. Light was good, darkness evil, and like many such underground sanctuaries Wookey acquired its mythical Hell's Ladder, a steep stone passageway leading to the mouth of hell itself.

However, rather than leading us to hell, such sanctuaries of dim light can help us to develop psychic and sometimes prophetic powers, as perhaps the witch did before us. When we move away from the light and the noise, the outer world loses its power and our energies switch to the inner world, in which we can gain enhanced awareness to carry back and use in everyday life.

Dark Places and Psychic Powers

The dark places of nature – deep forests, caves, mountains at night, ancient cromlechs and barrow tombs – are natural repositories of psychic power where earth energies flow uninterrupted. Especially powerful are those energy centres that are enclosed, such as caves or the rock crevasses enclosing subterranean wells. These form incubators of ancient earth energies that flowed millions of years before humans walked the Earth and will flow as long as the Earth exists.

These centres of stillness and silence help us to connect with our own still centre wherein resides the spark of divinity we all possess. This essential self is not bound by the limits of time, but flows backwards through the darkness into the past and forwards to the future ocean of unformed potential.

Our ancestors were closer to dark nature than many of us are today. Without modern transport journeys could take days or even weeks. Our forebears would travel on unlit tracks or over tracts of moorland, often sleeping on deserted hillsides, sheltering in caves or in woods at night. Thus they naturally absorbed psychic energy that enabled them to connect with unseen realms and become open to the voices of the night.

Dark places in the natural world are also containers of stored human wisdom, the knowledge and impressions of people who have visited such spots over the millennia, and the early peoples who once inhabited the caves and drew water from wells that seemed to lead to the Underworld itself. This wisdom is etched in the rocks, the crags and the deep underground streams. It is released when our feet, our hands and our inner spirit make contact with the womb of the hidden Earth Mother through the natural psychometric or psychic powers of touch we all possess.

Visiting or carrying out rituals at these power sources, either at night or in the natural dimness of the setting, enables us to absorb some of this knowledge. In doing so, we can kindle our own dormant psychic and prophetic powers.

Spending an hour in a dark outdoor place helps us to connect with our intuitive and invariably accurate inner voice. Traditionally, the inner voice was regarded as the wisdom of deities or angels, channelled into our minds when external stimuli have almost ceased. Channelling wisdom from higher sources has become popular over the last ten years. *Divus* or *diva*, the Latin word from which the word 'divination' derives, means 'god' or 'goddess'. I believe this is the god or goddess within us and so this inspiration could be regarded as a manifestation of the divine spark we all possess.

Dark Places and Prophetic Powers

A number of the oracular centres of prophecy in the ancient Greek and Roman worlds were in caves. The Oracle herself was originally a priestess of the Earth Mother, from whom she received her insights. In return for offerings she would make prophecies, often in cryptic terms.

The Roman Sibyl or prophetess at Cumae, for example, derived her authority from the Anatolian mother goddess Cybele or Kybele, whose name means 'cave-dweller'. She wrote prophecies on leaves in her cave and then opened the door so that the wind would scatter them and the questioners would have to catch them and piece the wisdom together for themselves.

Consulting the Oracle at ancient sites frequently involved underground journeys through dark narrow passages to a cave where the oracular priestess resided. Sometimes the seeker would receive direct insight from the deity. For example, at the Oracle of Trophonius at Lebadea in Boeotia, after bathing ritually in the River Erkynas, the seeker climbed down into the oracular cave at night by means of a ladder and then passed through a narrow dark passage, to remain alone in an inner cave in total darkness until wisdom came, either as a dream or as a vision from a deity.

Wisdom might also be sought from deceased relatives or sages by going to the mouth of the Underworld, where the oracular priestess would act as a trance medium. Recent information in the book *Discovering the Oracle of the Dead* by Robert Temple, a British-American scholar of ancient history, has suggested that these visits to the gates of Hades might have actually taken place. Temple identifies the entrance to Hades beneath the small seaside resort of Baia, a few miles west of Naples, close to Cumae. Here in the dark, hot, tomb-like atmosphere of an inner cavern, seekers would experience visions of their deceased relatives and hear their voices channelled through the oracular priestess.

Sensory Deprivation and Heightened Awareness

Journeys into darkness and silence created genuine states of altered awareness. Chanting, the burning of incense and rituals helped to ease the transition. Finally, total darkness took away the marker points of the everyday world and ordered reality. Time lost meaning and as the outer physical world disappeared so the inner psychic timeless sphere became the organising principle of a different reality.

Ancient Irish literature tells of Druidic rituals involving similar forms of sensory deprivation to induce prophecy in dreams, trance or at the moment when after a period of prolonged darkness light came flooding in.

At the Tarb-feis, a sacrificial bull-feast often associated with the midwinter celebrations, after the ritual slaughter of a white bull, a Druid or Druidess would chew some of the tough meat to set up a rhythmic physical activity and then wrap themselves in the bull hide to induce visions in sleep. Other accounts tell of the Druid or Druidess sleeping beneath a waterfall wrapped in the bull hide so that the intense sound would flood the consciousness.

We can adapt these ancient methods to allow our inner voice to speak to us and to receive inspirational words of prophecy. Fortunately we shall not need the bull skin.

Finding a Special Dark Place in Nature

First you need to find or create your oracular sanctuary. You may be lucky enough to live close to a place of sanctity where it is always twilight or which you can visit after dark.

Your place will reflect slightly different energies according to the season, the weather and the phase of the Moon. On occasions you may sit there in the velvet darkness for hours, while at other times you may only manage ten minutes. Over the months you will imbue the place with your special essence and can in return draw from the accumulated energies whenever you need inspiration.

For more regular work, adapt a dark corner in the garden. Improvise by planting bushes in an urban garden. Use a beach shelter to shut out street lights or use a mask or blindfold. On a balcony, sit on a cushion between plant tubs holding a stone you have brought back from a magical country site.

If necessary, sit near an open window in an apartment, or, like the Druids, cover yourself, in this case with a blanket, to create total darkness. If noise is a problem in your urban sanctuary, use earplugs or an unconnected headset.

Evoking Oracular Wisdom from Within

At first you may need a stimulus to get your inner wisdom flowing and help it to connect with the universal pool of knowledge.

- Choose a book of wisdom – the I Ching, the Bible, the Koran, the works of Shakespeare or a huge book of poetry.

- Open it at any page and begin reading about halfway down the left-hand page at the first complete sentence or phrase. Read no more than two lines.

- Read the lines until you have memorised them then close the book.

- In the darkness visualise the words written in lights or flames across the darkness. Recite them as a mantra over and over in your mind, gradually slowing the words until they trail into silence.

- Wait. At first you will hear just the lines.

- Gradually the stream of words will grow and become spontaneous.

- Initially, do not attempt to record or analyse the words, just practise tapping into the stream of wisdom.

- When you feel confident that your oracular flow is established, you can try taping the words using a battery-powered recorder.

- Listen to the recording again in the darkness just before you go to sleep and the wisdom may continue to flow in your dreams.

- Record your words in your Book of Shadows and carefully note the date. In time your words will guide your personal life and shed wisdom on current or future political or environmental situations.

Work with a variety of written sources. Some will prove more effective in evoking your own oratory than others.

Another method is to choose a Tarot card at random, focus on the picture, memorise the details and then superimpose that in the darkness and let words flow.

While you are building up these skills, spend weekends or holidays in quiet places whenever you can. It may be a campsite you visit regularly, a particular tree in urban woodland, a waterfall where the brilliant white water contrasts with the deep shadows of the rocks or a hilltop from which you can watch twilight descending over the land.

Working with Dark Sacred Places

An individual's sacred core can be confirmed and enhanced through association with an established sacred place. This is especially true at night in the stillness and silence after the tourists have gone home.

Every land has its sacred sites. Some are unmarked by a monument and you may instinctively be drawn to a spot though it is not an official sacred place. If you study the local folklore there may be legends of giants, dragons or fairies in the area, symbols through which people in the past have tried to explain what they feel (*see also pages 175–6*). One explanation may be that a number of ley or psychic energy lines converge at the point. This focal power may have been amplified by the rituals and wishes of people who have come to pray or leave offerings at this spot over the millennia.

Some sacred sites are very close to towns or are in suburban settings. Check your local history for these mythical centres. Look for names such as Dragon's Leap or Druid's Circle. The advantage of these more informal sites of sanctity is that they can be visited at any time on dark winter days, at twilight or before dawn.

However, there are also officially recognised places of sanctity that are open even at night and in the depths of winter. Ones I have visited include Amesbury Ring in Wiltshire, Ales Stenar in Skane in southern Sweden, a magnificent ship formation of ancient stones on the cliffs, and the huge Saffron Walden labyrinth in Essex. This is the most ancient turf labyrinth in England and one of the largest, with 17 rings and a diameter of 132 feet, which means a walk of a mile to the centre. In America and Canada, a number of open-air labyrinths are already becoming acknowledged as sacred sites and are also very accessible.

Barrows and Burial Mounds

Long barrows and ancient burial mounds can be found throughout Europe and Scandinavia. Like other indigenous burial sites throughout the world they were not intended just as graves, but as centres for celebrating the afterlife, seeking the wisdom of the ancestors and experiencing otherworldly visions.

Our ancestors celebrated death and would hold ceremonies in or near tombs to honour the dead as part of the continuing community.

Druids or Druidesses would lie in a long barrow from dusk till dawn in total darkness, to be woken at dawn by light flooding into the East-facing entrance and creating a flash of powerful psychic awareness that could give visions of the future.

Working in Long Barrows and Old Tombs

Choose a place where you feel comfortable. Some people, for example, find ancient Egyptian tombs or pyramids oppressive, though a number are known for their powerful healing energies. If you do feel too enclosed in a long barrow or tomb, you can work in a cave or shady place near a burial ground.

If you time your visit for late afternoon in the winter months or the evening in the summer, you can leave the dark place before nightfall. Sit, stand or kneel alone or with a friend in the darkness and allow the peace of the past to flow over and through you, connecting you in an unbroken line to early peoples, even in lands hundreds of miles from home.

Even on an official tour you can often miss part of the commentary to spend time in a quiet recess, as I did at Wookey. It is not the time but the quality of the experience that is important and you can recreate it in your mind later in another quiet place.

Visions of the past will emerge spontaneously. These may be of personal past lives or the world of your ancestors. You may also connect with the people who built the barrows or who worshipped there, perhaps with a figure of similar age and personality.

If you wish, carry out a brief private ritual using a crystal, a flower or a tiny charm as a focus. Visualise the energies being absorbed by the darkness of the earth, where your needs and wishes can grow and bear fruit over the next weeks and months. Underground work is potent for slow-germinating wishes or to leave behind old sorrows. Leave the symbol charged by your thoughts in the tomb or bury a banishing wish close to the path on the way back to the road.

My favourite source of dark power is West Kennett long barrow, which is situated on a high chalk ridge near the artificially created Mother Goddess mound Silbury Hill, not far from Avebury stones in Wiltshire. It is the largest chambered long barrow in Britain and is in an area where many psychic ley energy lines converge. It is easily accessible but almost always deserted, and many times I have heard the voices of the past whispering messages of peace and seen the shadows of the earth essences that have made the tomb their home.

Dolmens

Even more magnificent are the huge portal or stone gateway tombs, also called dolmens. They can be found throughout Western Europe, the Mediterranean and Scandinavia, and their inner chambers can be visited and used as a focus for private ritual and meditation.

Cromlechs

Cromlechs consist of three or more standing stones capped by a large monolith (single stone). The dead would be buried in an earthen mound beneath the cromlech. These structures were built between 4,000 and 5,000 years ago and erosion has caused many of them to sink right into the mound, so they appear like a giant's altar or table. Sometimes the earth itself has eroded away.

The Pentre Ifan cromlech in Pembrokeshire, Wales, was used for Druidic initiation, the would-be Druids spending time in the darkness of the tomb/womb before being spiritually reborn and emerging into the light.

Andalusian Dolmens

My own special dolmens are in Andalusia in Spain on the northern outskirts of the town of Antequera. The most impressive is the Cueva de Menga, its roof formed by massive stone slabs, among them a 180-ton monolith dating from around 2500 BC. If you stand at the entrance and look upwards you can see a huge rock on a cliff in the shape of a slumbering giant, whose table the cromlech forms. The Sun rises over the head of this rock at the Summer Solstice and on this day only, the first rays penetrate the burial chamber.

When the monument is closed there are mysterious guardians who appear and let in visitors. When I went an old man seemingly materialised out of thin air and opened the dolmens for my family. For extra money it may be possible to spend time in the tombs alone. Do not be deterred by the unimpressive setting of the dolmens.

Newgrange

One of the best known passage graves is at Newgrange in the Boyne Valley, in County Meath not far from Dublin in Ireland. Originally built about 3100 BC, it was once called Grian Uaigh, 'Cave of the Sun God'.

Newgrange is close to Tara, the sacred hill and palace of the Tuatha de Danaan, the Celtic hero gods and goddesses, later called the fairy folk (*see page 173*). Newgrange has symbols inscribed on the circle stones recording highly accurate ancient astronomical calculations, as well as Goddess spirals within the tomb.

Within the chamber in Celtic times the high priestess stood in the darkness on Winter Solstice morning, pouring water over a spiral on the wall and making incantations for the Sun to bring rebirth to the world.

Wherever you live in the world, you can research the myths behind these ancient burial places, the tales of Sun gods who slumbered there at nightfall or died at the midwinter festival to be reborn as shafts of light penetrated the tomb. The world over you can enter the portals of the past and overcome our modern taboos about the dead, as you feel the sanctity and promises of renewal within.

Glens, Pools and Waterfalls

Water sites are invariably magical. Though I knew little of the psychic world when I stood near the foot of Niagara Falls, I was overwhelmed by the contrast between the dark steps I had climbed down and the brilliant roaring of the water that revealed thousands of sparkling dancing water nymphs and the booming voice of the native water god. Being at the time a very sensible teacher married to an even more sensible civil engineer, I assumed it was a trick of the light or the wine in the Falls Motel, but now, more than 20 years on, I know better.

The smallest waterfall or dark pool can be equally magical, whether one of those deep Black Forest elf king pools, a desert oasis under the chill night air, a haunted Australian billabong or your garden pond with a tiny water pump.

One of the most beautiful water sites I know is St Nectan's Glen and waterfall, between Boscastle and Tintagel in Cornwall. Not surprisingly, the glen is known for fairy sightings and though you can't gain access at night, it is never truly light there, even on the sunniest day. You are enveloped in moss-green twilight with silence broken only by the birds. At the foot of the falls are shrines in caverns to the Earth Mother, called locally the Lady of the Waterfall.

By reading guide books or looking on the Internet you can find countless similar sites. Even hot lands have their shady places.

Night Scrying in Pools and Rivers

Scrying is using a reflective surface to stimulate and amplify images from deep within your mind into, in this case, water. Night or darkness scrying is especially effective because there is only a small area of light contrasting with the large expanse of darkness around it. You may be lucky enough to find a dark pool overhung by trees where even in sunshine there are deep shadows on the water. Best of all, scry on a moonlit night where the light shines on the water.

You need only a small pool such as a garden pond. On a moon-less night, shine a torch on the water, moving it in circles for effect, or position outdoor candles or torches to reflect small circles of rippling light. A lake with a fountain of the kind where there are a few coloured lights in the water also works well. Shallow rivers can also be a good focus. Ones running through town with the odd street light are remarkably evocative.

If there is no suitable water source, substitute a dark glass bowl and fill it with water. Add floating candles and sit in the darkness.

- You may wish to begin by invoking your special guardian or your own higher powers to assist and protect you as you work.

- Ask a question, and if the water source is unmoving, stir it with a stick so you get slight rippling; focus on the light on the dark water through half-closed eyes.

- If you are new to water scrying, as soon as you stir the water or focus on a ripple, say aloud the first image or words that come into your mind. This prevents your conscious mind from intruding and rationalising or telling you that you can't see anything.

- Continue to focus and speak until you have three or four images.

- As you become more confident in the accuracy of your scrying, you can take longer to study each image and build up pictures or scenes.

- When you get home or into the light, draw what you saw or heard in your Book of Shadows, or write it down. Scrying can induce words spoken by your inner voice, your night guardian or special angel. Also record any impressions or feelings that you experienced while scrying.

- Sit by candlelight and allow the images to form again in your mind's eye. Repeat the words aloud and recreate the feelings.

- As you do this, you may instantly understand the significance of your night visions. If not, weave them into a story of a journey or an adventure. The outcome of the story and the fate of the hero or heroine will indicate a future path or decision. The beauty of the story-telling method of analysis is that as it is your story, you can test out different endings until one feels right for your own life.

- You may like to look at the list of dream images (*see pages 200–8*), as dream meanings are almost identical to those of scrying. However, it is perhaps most helpful to start your own symbol dictionary, adding to it as you use any form of divination. You may decide to combine the dream and scrying symbols in an all-purpose A–Z.

Subterranean Magical and Healing Waters

Many caves that have become recognised sacred sites have an underground stream or river flowing through them. From early times it was believed that this water came from deep within the womb of Mother Earth and because it was enclosed within a cave, itself an Earth Mother symbol, it was filled with great healing power.

Some of these subterranean waters have been incorporated into church and cathedral crypts. The crypt of Chartres cathedral near Paris, with its Black Earth Mother statue and subterranean well, formed part of the Christian pilgrimage of medieval times. It was built on the Druids' subterranean grotto and well, dedicated to the Druidic Virgin, who, it was prophesied, would give birth to the saviour.

A number of underground wells have survived in their original form, for example Sancreed Well near Penzance. Even in summer you can experience night mystery there as you descend steep steps into the earth where a tiny well pool remains. Because it is off the beaten track you should not be disturbed and can spend time scrying into the water.

Working with Healing Wells

- In a church or cathedral, head for the crypt and look for a well, even if the guide book does not mention one. Most cathedrals have sacred water sources either beneath the cathedral itself or in a well house in the grounds close by. These waters will be incredibly ancient and have healing properties, which in Christian times were dedicated to a saint or the Virgin Mary.

- When you find a well, whether in the depths of the earth or a cathedral, gaze down into it, close your eyes, open them and blink. You may see a momentary image or scene in the spot of light in the water below or may hear prophetic words from the Earth Mother herself.

- You can also draw upon the undiluted healing energy flowing deep in the earth.

- Focus on the bottom of the shaft and ask for healing, either for yourself or for someone else.

- Leave an offering close to the well or money for its upkeep.

Caves

I began by describing the caves at Wookey Hole, where I feel particularly connected with Earth power. The darkness and silence of caves make them natural conductors of psychic night vision or hearing, more commonly called clairvoyance and clairaudience. Clairvoyance can take the form of internal or external images or whole scenes that are related either to the future or to a distant place or another dimension, while clairaudience involves hearing sounds from other times and places or the voices of the deceased.

These powers are more easily accessible in the absence of light stimuli, but once they are fully evolved you will find they operate effectively during the daytime. Both are central to prophecy and indeed to spiritual development generally, enabling you to tune into other dimensions more rapidly.

You can work with your own favourite caves, either in your region or when you go on holiday. If you holiday in a place with cliffs, you may locate a cave where you can be totally private. Check the tides and ask locals about the speed of the currents before you begin your venture.

Among my favourite caves are the mystical Cueva del Tresor (Treasure Caves) near Malaga in Andalusia in Spain. Because you are able to wander around without a guide, you can carry out simple meditation or rituals in them. There is a well in one of the caves and drawings that indicate the caves have been used for worship from Palaeolithic times.

The place where I feel the night power most within the cave complex is the Santuario de la Diosa Noctiluca, the prehistoric sanctuary consecrated to the goddess Noctiluca, who represented life, death and fertility. She was goddess of the night and the Moon. Her sanctuary dates from Neolithic times, perhaps earlier, and in its base have been found the remains of sacrificed animals.

Your Inner Cave

Though the energies are most powerful in these natural subterranean places, you can transfer the sensation and the spiritual
stillness to less tranquil aspects of your life. With practice you can
evoke an 'inner cave' in the noisiest, most harshly lit office or train
simply by closing your eyes and mentally drawing the soothing
blackness all around you.

I developed this technique almost by accident in the shadowy
cathedral of Bayeux in northern France. I arrived late on a winter's
afternoon and the cathedral was almost in darkness except for the last
rays of low sunlight filtering through the heavy windows. Indeed, I
walked the labyrinth in the Chapter House by the light of the custo-
dian's torch, as there were no lights at all in that part of the cathedral.

The crypt was illuminated on a timer switch and I realised that
by standing close to the switch I was able to remain in total
darkness for several minutes, then briefly illuminate the medieval
fresco on the pillars, the painted angels playing bagpipes, an
accordion and even a bombard, a flute-type instrument popular in
that region of France.

I gazed at the angels intently in the brief period of light, then
visualised them in the darkness. By alternating brief periods of light
with increasing periods of darkness, the visualised image became as
powerful and three-dimensional as the real one.

I experienced a similar phenomenon spontaneously when
emerging from the shadowy interior of a basilica in Zagorsk, not far
from Moscow. There was a sudden overwhelming flash of
brilliance, etching on the whiteness a vision of the beautiful gold
and jewelled icons I had been peering at through the dimness and
the smoke of thick incense. I saw doorways into the icons, dark
winding passageways going inwards to a dark jewelled centre, and I
had a sudden flash of insight that I had lost something precious –
myself – in a marriage that I desperately wanted to succeed. I later
found out that my husband was unfaithful even then, but I needed
so much to be loved and to be accepted into the comfortable
middle-class world he represented that I closed my eyes to his
coldness and his need for control. So I willingly went back into the
dark passages of my life. I knew nothing of the psychic world then
and was quite frightened. I did not realise I was seeing with my
night or clairvoyant eye.

Using Your Night Eye

Clairvoyance operates through the power of this inner, night or third eye that lies in the centre of the brow just above the physical eyes. Using your night eye is perhaps the single most important skill in recreating a place of sanctity in the everyday world.

You already began using this technique when evoking your inner prophecy (*see page 150*) when you visualised the words of wisdom set against the darkness. Now you will use an external stimulus to trigger your inner powers.

This flashbulb technique involves briefly illuminating a dark place to imprint it on your psyche as if on a photographic plate. This imprints the scene on your inner eye, to be projected whenever you need a sanctuary.

Of course you will not just be using psychic vision, but all your psychic antennae. In your mind you will build up the sound of dripping water, the smell of damp moss or the feel of an icy stalactite.

Though I have called this exercise 'Creating Your Inner Cave', you can use the stimulus of an actual dolmen, a deep pool or a forest glade.

Creating Your Inner Cave

- Take a torch with you and sit or stand in the dark place. Stare intently into the blackness and focus on the different aspects of the setting one by one as your vision adjusts to the darkness.

- Switch your torch on and off almost instantly, like the flashbulb action on a camera. This concentrated light, like the Druids coming out into the light from the long barrow, imprints the scene in your mind and as a bonus may give you sudden insights or even visions of the future.

- Recreate the flash of light in your mind as you project outwards the image of yourself and your cave or dark place. Imprint the momentary clear vision on to the physically indistinct features.

- Repeat the first three steps until you can see the cave as clearly in the darkness as with your torch.

- When you return home, repeat step three. Continue creating your cave mentally until you can recall it anywhere, any time.

You can use your inner cave to enclose yourself in psychic protection as well as to create an oasis of calm. You can use it anywhere – at work when it becomes too noisy or frantic, at home to help you to relax or sleep, wherever you want to meditate or you need a quiet space but there is no physical refuge. I have even used it on a crowded train when I have to work when I reach the end of the journey.

In time other dark and sacred places can be recreated in your mind, so that even on the busiest street you walk through moss-green twilight beside a bubbling stream.

9

Creatures of the Night

We talk of the silence of the night, yet it is full of sounds. If you stand in the countryside you may hear the hooting of owls, the chirping of cicadas, the barking of foxes, the howling of wolves, the melody of the nightingale, the snuffling of hedgehogs in a pile of leaves. There are silent creatures, too – bats swooping with their barely perceptible whirr and call pitched too high for the human ear. The night is alive even in the centre of a town with creatures whose secret world is vibrant with energies that we can absorb to empower ourselves. Because night creatures are hidden and secret, they can help us to uncover our own hidden potential and release the fears and frustrations we hold in our shadow or night selves.

It is said that the creatures of the night are the alter egos of the daytime creatures. The jaguar in Central and South America is called the Dark Sun King because his spots glitter like the stars at night. He is the night aspect of the daytime predator the Light Sun King, the eagle. The hawk, another daytime hunter, is replaced in the dark sky by the owl. Even the butterfly has its night-time shadow, the moth.

The senses of the night creatures are especially acute. The owl, for example, has such finely tuned hearing that it can identify the precise location of its prey in total darkness while it flies silently high above the fields.

In many ages and cultures shamans have worked with animals

and have been depicted with bird or animal heads. The powerful transference of animal power to humans can both fill us with energy and instinctual force and be very protective as the chosen creature extends its fierceness or ability to evade capture. These qualities can be as useful in the urban jungle as in the wild.

Becoming Familiar with the World of the Night Creatures

There many ways in which you can learn about creatures of the night. Increasingly, wildlife centres throughout the world are offering night-time walks or studies. Many animal and bird conservation parks have night houses where you can walk through a dimly lit area and observe the animals through a two-way shaded mirror so that they are unaware of your presence. The best wildlife centres have cameras positioned to see natural underground setts and burrows. Alternatively, there are excellent wildlife videos of animals and birds in their nocturnal or underground habitats. You can also erect a bat box in your garden and leave areas of untended undergrowth to encourage small creatures.

The fiercer creatures of the night are predators. In very hot countries or deserts the coolness of the night is the natural time to be out hunting for food. Desert foxes live in burrows beneath the ground in the intense heat of the day and come out at night. In temperate climes, too, burrowing creatures like the North American opossum and the European badger emerge at twilight to hunt.

If you are unfamiliar with night creatures, it is worth spending time studying them as this can greatly enhance your understanding in magical work.

Power Animals of the Night

A number of indigenous peoples, for example the Australian Aboriginals and Native Americans, develop kinship with a particular species of animal. Some Australian Aboriginals claim descent from a nocturnal creature in its ideal or archetypal form at the time of creation. Among the Native North Americans, an adolescent may adopt the name of a particular species after their first sojourn or Vision Quest in the wilderness. The creature may have come near during the night and communicated telepathically.

Shamans sometimes use the spirit form of particularly fierce or swift night creatures, for example the jaguar or black panther, as their steed and for protection in other realms.

Amulets made from the claw, beak or teeth of one of these creatures are worn or carried to endow the wearer with the creature's protection. When empowered as talismans by chanting or ritual, they attract the strength or qualities of the creature.

Finding Your Personal Night Power Animal

You may already have a personal power animal or bird that perhaps has appeared in dreams or is a species you have been fascinated by since childhood.

If your usual power animal roams in daylight, you may find it helpful to connect with a nocturnal creature as well, especially if you are nervous of darkness, if you frequently work or travel in darkness or if you need reserves of power at a critical time in your life. Nocturnal and burrowing creatures also bring energy and reserves of strength in the long winter months or during a personal emotional wintertime.

If no night icon seems relevant, spend time in the countryside at night or watching nocturnal creatures in conservation parks. Select a wildlife video of a night-time forest at random and you will find that before long your chosen creature will appear in a dream or an unusual context.

Absorbing the Protection of Your Night Icon

Where our ancestors would have wrapped themselves in the skins of their creatures to absorb their invulnerability as well as to ride their spirits in astral travel, in a more ecologically aware time you may prefer to buy a synthetic fur blanket or rug for your night place or to cover you when you go camping. Equally, you may prefer to carry a wooden or silver protective amulet of your chosen creature rather than an amulet made from a claw, beak or tooth.

You can also increase the connection between yourself and the hidden animal world by setting pictures, photographs or ceramic models of nocturnal animals or birds on your night altar. For even deeper affinity, craft your favourite night-dweller from clay or pottery. This is a particularly effective way of drawing their strengths to you.

As you sit quietly, play CDs of the animal and bird calls of the night and imagine yourself in the jungle or woodland or on a wild hillside where the wolves call. Picture yourself as your chosen creature. If a bird, feel wings sprouting.

You can visualise your nocturnal power animal before a meeting or confrontation when you know you may experience malice or unfair criticism. Protective night creatures are especially valuable if you find yourself alone at night locking up your workplace, on a deserted railway station, in a crowded potentially dangerous urban setting or having to walk home along a dark road and unlock the front door alone. Your power wolf or jaguar beside you will ensure you do not give off potential victim vibes and will enfold you in their protection.

You can also adopt the name of your power creatures as your secret power name for invocations or ritual, for example: 'I, Mother Wolf, ask that . . .'

Increasing the Talismanic Power

This will empower your symbol so that it attracts the qualities of your permanent night animal or bird into your life as well as offering protection. You can also empower symbols with a creature whose strengths you most need at a particular time or in a specific recurring situation or relationship issue.

- Sprinkle salt around a picture or model, encircle it with nine rings of the smoke of myrrh or mimosa incense, pass it over the flame of a dark red candle and finally sprinkle it with water in which a tiger's eye or rutilated quartz has been soaked for eight hours.

- As you do so, recite as a continuous chant the creature's name and any specific strength.

- End by calling your creature to aid you. Increase the speed and intensity of the words and movement so that you end on a climax of focused power. You can make the chant as elaborate or as simple as you wish.

Creatures of the Night

If you do not already relate to a power creature, here is a list of some that have worked for people I know. As you read the list you may recognise one of which you have dreamed or with which you feel kinship. Learn all you can about your power creature and write about it in your Book of Shadows.

Bat

The bat is one of the most magical and misunderstood creatures of the night because of its legendary association with the mythical vampire. In fact of the thousand species of bat only three suck the blood of animals and they live in South America.

African legend tells that it was the bat that first brought darkness into the world. He had been entrusted with carrying a covered basket to the Moon, which until then shone brightly every night, making it as light as day. However, the bat left the basket unattended and a curious monkey lifted the lid, thus releasing the darkness, which the bat has ever since tried to catch.

From medieval times right through to the end of the 17th century in Europe and Scandinavia the bat was feared as a witch's familiar spirit or even the Devil himself.

Because some bats roost during the daytime in caves and ruined buildings, they have come to symbolise the spirit world. The Egyptian fruit bat, for example, was discovered living in sealed ancient tombs and temples.

Use bat power for exploring and overcoming illogical fears you have buried within you, and for overcoming fears of the dark and of spiritual phenomena that cannot be explained in material terms.

Cat

The cat is one of the most universal and ancient creatures of the night. In ancient Egypt, the fertility and lunar goddess Bast was depicted with a cat's head or sometimes as a cat, called Bastet (*see page 211*). Sacred cats were kept in temples dedicated to her and on their death were mummified and adorned with jewellery and buried as offerings by rich petitioners.

In Buddhist temples in Burma it was believed that the priests returned as the sacred temple cats. Cats accompanied both the Viking goddess of love Freyja and the Celtic Crone Cerridwen. Freyja's black cats pulled her chariot.

Because cats roamed the night and their eyes glow in the dark, they were considered to be a form witches assumed when they gathered at night, or to be the spirits of dead witches.

Use your cat power for protection of your home and family, for magical energies to bring thought into reality, for the rebirth of hopes and dreams, and for increased clairvoyance.

Jaguar

Jaguars live in the northern and central areas of South America, especially in the forests around the Amazon and in central and southern Mexico. In the deeply forested regions some have developed dark coats through which the spots faintly shine. Similarly dark-coated leopards are found in the rainforests in South East Asia.

In South America it is told that the jaguar taught humans to use bows and arrows and gave them cooked meat from his own fire. But men stole the fire and killed his wife and so he now lives alone in deep forests and is their enemy. The Mayans, however, considered the Jaguar god to be very protective and to guard villages. He was called the Earth Father, Lord of all the forest.

Use your jaguar power for courage, for travelling safely at night, for shapeshifting into different modes of thinking when you need to adapt, for astral travel and for hunting down new opportunities.

Moth

Like butterflies, moths are primarily a symbol of reincarnation and regeneration, because of their ability to metamorphose from egg to caterpillar to moth.

The concept of moths as souls in transit, especially those who die at night, is found in a number of cultures including the Australian Aboriginal and the Chinese. The attraction of moths to the light is regarded as an attempt to make the transition to the spirit world. As a species that has existed for about 60 million years, the moth is not surprisingly also a symbol of immortality.

Use your moth power for transcending the mundane, for

spiritual renewal, for astral travel and making contact with other dimensions, and when seeking fulfilment whatever the price.

Nightingale

The nightingale is a truly magical bird whose song can be heard in the stillness of the night.

One myth tells that on a wintry night a nightingale soothed the restless baby Jesus to sleep with his singing. As a result Mary blessed the bird and declared his song should be the sweetest of all the birds.

Another legend says that the first lily-of-the-valley loved the nightingale, but because she was so shy she hid in the long grass to listen to his song. The nightingale became lonely and at last said he would no longer sing unless the lily-of-the-valley bloomed every May for all to see. Now when the moonlight shines upon the lily-of-the-valley's delicate white bells, the nightingale sings his sweetest and the returning song of the tiny bells can be heard in the stillness.

Use your nightingale power for bringing beauty and harmony to your life, for spreading joy to others and for all situations where the voice of peace and grace is needed to melt coldness or to bring reconciliation to warring factions.

Owl

Though not all owls are nocturnal, magically and mythologically they are creatures of the night. When they swoop, wings outstretched and huge eyes wide, across the face of the Moon or pale against the darkness, they resemble ghosts, and they are associated with spirits in a number of cultures.

Among the Maoris of New Zealand owls are revered as guardian spirits of the community and wise ancestors. In ancient Greece, Athene, goddess of wisdom, had the owl as her symbol, as did her Roman counterpart Minerva. In a number of other cultures, including the Native North American, the owl was a wise teacher, especially of traditions.

To the Celts the owl and the owl goddess were associated with the Moon. The owl was the bird of the Crone, an association that was later transferred to banshees, especially in Scotland. A banshee might appear as an owl flapping at the window of the dying. This accords with the role of the owl in warning of death, since an owl heralded the death of the Roman emperors Julius Caesar, Augustus, Commodus Aurelius and Agrippa.

Use owl power for acquiring wisdom, for developing your own powerful inner voice that can advise and warn, and for welcoming personal ancestors into your dreams and meditation.

Wolf

The wolf is regarded as a particularly wise teacher in the Native North American tradition. In other cultures too it is revered not only for its skill in hunting but also as a pack creature with intense loyalty to its kin.

Fiercely protective, a mother wolf is said to be able to defeat even a tiger in defence of her young. She is famed both in myth and in chronicled cases in India for raising abandoned human infants. In Classical myth Lupa the wolf goddess suckled the infants Romulus and Remus who founded Rome. The wolf is a messenger and a guide to otherworldly realms, especially at the time of the full Moon.

Use your wolf power when you need to be fierce in the defence of your clan, be they at home or work, or to promote loyalty among a group of individuals. Invoke it above all for your own untamed connection with nature.

Shapeshifting and Power Animals of the Night

Shamans around the world believe it is possible to merge with different birds and animals and see the world through their eyes, soaring in the skies or burrowing in the earth. Because of their ability to walk through the darkness undetected, night creatures are especially potent for this 'shapeshifting' work.

The shapeshifting process would seem to work through the merging of auras or psychic energy fields. Just as you are able to take in the energies from the auras of planetary bodies, so you can absorb the psychic energies of your chosen night creature and emit their signals. So, for example, in a potentially confrontational situation you could either move unobtrusively out of danger as a mouse or cat, or face down the attacker as the fierce night jaguar.

You can also gain different perspectives on the world by moving in spirit form as an owl or a bat, for example. What is more, you can enhance your psychic senses of vision or hearing as you work with the heightened instinctive powers of the night creatures.

Indeed, you can work your way through many species of nocturnal animal and build up a repository of increased awareness so that even in the daytime you are closely in touch with your intuition. This 'animal cunning' helps you to sense if a person is trustworthy, an offer advantageous or the time right to go to a place or confide in a person.

On a higher level you can absorb the knowledge of ancient times from Egyptian tomb bats or Athene's little owl as you tap into the clan genes of your chosen species.

How to Shapeshift

- Gather together material about two or three species. You might like to begin with night creatures you can observe locally or in a nearby conservation park.

- Initially the animal's physical presence is very valuable in making the psychic link between the animal and human aura. The domestic cat is a good preliminary subject as it is easily observed at close proximity.

- Choose your first night animal. If there are a number of similar animals or birds kept in the same place, one in particular may resonate with you or come close to you.

- Observe the animal's physical characteristics – eyes, wings, movement and distinctive markings – and visualise the softness of the fur, the breath. At conservation parks or on the Internet you can find information about how a particular species sees the world, which may be completely differently from the human field of vision. If the creature is not in its native habitat, find out all you can about its lair or burrow, the kind of terrain it lives in and the climate, the food it eats and where it obtains water.

- Gather any myths or folklore about the species so that you can understand the essential spirit that is often expressed through such legends.

- Allow all this information to work its way into your sub-conscious mind and take root by focusing on an actual image of the creature just before you go to sleep.

- After a week or so observe the creature again, this time focusing on the area around the head where the aura is most visible. Birds often have silvery grey auras and small domesticated creatures brown or pink ones. Cats tend to exude mainly purple and fierce predators dark red. Animals' auras tend to vary less in colour than those of humans, though domestic animals do become more in tune with the auras of their owners. Wilder animals tend to have the colour of their species, though a kind one may also display pink or green, especially a mother with young.

- If you want to know more, go where there is a variety of creatures, stare at one of each species, close your eyes, open them, blink and you will see the main colour of the aura. You can record these in your Book of Shadows.

- Before beginning to merge your own energy field with that of the animal, hold one of your protective night crystals (*see page 30*) in each hand and ask that only positive energies will enter your field. Obsidian is especially good for animal work.

- Visualise your own aura moving closer and merging with that of the creature. Breathe gently and rhythmically to blend the coloured energies so that they swirl around you both.

- Now imagine the boundaries surrounding both outlines melting and step within the creature's space so that you can see through their eyes and hear through their ears. Now you can see an antelope fixed in your glittering headlight vision on the plain or hear the rustling of a mouse in the undergrowth a hundred feet below.

- Harmonise your breathing pattern with that of the animal.

- Set the creature in motion, soaring, running or bounding, and merge psychically with their rhythm.

- When you are ready, recreate the separate boundaries between you and the creature and gently withdraw your own essence back into your body.

- At home sit in semi-darkness. Take a photograph or symbol of your animal or bird and stare at it intently for a few seconds.

- Enter the symbolic aura as you did when you were observing the real animal or bird.

- Once more see through its eyes, hear through its ears and build up an awareness of the habitat around you.

- Now move with the creature either through the physical world or through the skies into another dimension.

- When you have finished your journey, mentally separate your auras by recreating the separate outlines. Ease away slowly in your mind.

- Shake your fingers and feet and step out of your power creature, thanking them for your safe passage.

- Keep notes in your Book of Shadows of the sensations and any particularly vivid images. You may find that your spirit animal builds up a distinct personality and may impart the traditional wisdom of the clan.

- Do something positive for an individual member of your chosen species, or put out seeds for the wild birds.

With practice you can summon almost instantly any night form into which you can shapeshift to face challenges and become strong when you need to in the everyday world.

Mythical and Magical Creatures of the Night

Just as fascinating as nocturnal animals and birds are the magical creatures of myth and legend that live under hills, within ancient burial mounds or in deep caves, and emerge when darkness falls. Tales of these 'fairy folk' have been passed down from generation to generation.

Some people believe that fairies are no more than folk memories of small, less technologically advanced Neolithic tribes driven back by invading peoples who retreated to caves in the mountains. Others have suggested that the descendants of these tribes survived in the thick forests that covered Europe until the Middle Ages.

As late as the twelfth century, according to Gillian Tyndall, author of *A Handbook of Witches* (Arthur Barker, 1965), at Wolfpits in Suffolk it was recorded that a green-coloured boy and girl who could not speak the language suddenly appeared out of nowhere. They would eat nothing but beans and were very distressed. The boy died. It is not known what happened to the girl.

In the modern world factual reports of people seeing fairies have declined as fewer people cross remote tracts of land on foot at night and sleep under the stars. But whatever the hard facts, for generations magical energies have been perceived as fairy folk in wild lonely places after dark. Fairies appeared at night, it is argued, because that is the time when the Otherworld superimposes itself on the everyday world.

Under the Hollow Hill

Hollow hills are the traditional homes of the fey folk. Some of these naturally hollow places were used as burial mounds, and fairy sightings at these suggested that fairies were spirits of the dead. But others, like Glastonbury Tor in Somerset, were used for human worship. The natural warrens of tunnels and caves beneath the Tor, now inaccessible, were believed to lead to the Celtic Otherworld and in later myth were the route to fairyland. Gwynn ap Nudd, Gwynn the White Son of Night, who later was downgraded to a fairy king, guarded the entrance.

Myths about the fairy people may have started with the coming of Christianity, when the pagan deities were either demonised or reduced to the status of fairies like Gwynn. But they persisted right through into the 20th century and were of special interest to Victorians.

In Ireland, the most famous fairy court, the Daoine Sidh, was said to live under the hill of Tara (*see page 154*). Once called the Tuatha de Danaan of Ireland, in Celtic times they were children of the mother goddess Danu. The Tuatha de Danaan were credited with building the megaliths of Ireland, which are still seen as gateways to the world of fairy, and they were the guardians of the original Grail treasures.

As fairies they were believed to occupy subterranean palaces of gold and crystal, and tales of them were collected until early in the 20th century. Travellers would see open doorways of light beneath the hill and if a mortal entered there would be feasting, music and dancing. The mortal would be wooed by the fairy king or queen, returning to the human world years later after what seemed only a night away.

Fairies of Brittany

Though fairies appear in every land from Scandinavia and China to Africa and North America, the ultimate fey country is Brittany, which is often shrouded in mist, especially in the autumn and winter months. Brittany probably has more fairy sightings and tales that anywhere else, partly because it is still remote psychologically from the rest of France and was a refuge for so many Druid priests and priestesses from Britain.

The Corrigans, Breton maiden fairies dressed in white who were believed to be dispossessed pagan princesses or Druidesses, are said to dance at night around sacred fountains, in grottoes and woodland groves. They are hideously ugly in the daylight and so do not show their faces when the Sun shines.

There are also whole troops of smaller fairies, the *fées*, who live underground in tumuli, dolmens, menhirs or deep forests, and may be seen as shadowy forms at twilight. They are believed to be angels who remained neutral in the war in heaven, but then found the gates of heaven locked against them, so stayed on Earth and became diminished.

Also, until the beginning of the 20th century it was believed in Brittany that those who died resided with the fairies and at night would return to their former villages and homes to continue their work and daily lives while mortals slept.

Working with the Legendary Energies of the Fey

Fairies are to be found all over the world, from deserts and deep lakes to high mountains. If you read local folklore or legends, you will find details which may explain some of the things you have glimpsed out of the corner of your eye as you have camped or walked through isolated places. Not that all fairies live in the wilderness – children still report them even in urban back gardens.

If you visit a fairy place, or indeed a site with giant or witch legends, you will immediately sense strong Earth energies. A pendulum will spiral quite wildly. You can work with the fairies there and also work with the tree or lake spirits in dense woodland or dark places overshadowed by misty mountains. These are all enchanted spots where you can transform your desires and dreams into reality or hasten along slow-moving ventures.

In spite of highly embroidered myths, you will not sense evil in such places but rather a suppressed excitement as though the air were alive, even on the calmest day or deep in a cavern.

I am convinced from my own research that the light orbs or circles captured on camera in such places and attributed to spirit forms may be small concentrated globules of energy potential that in twilight or darkness we perceive as elves or fairies or even witches. Indeed, the wise women who lived in caves may have manipulated these energy bubbles in their magical workings.

When I stayed in a remote farmhouse south of Stockholm last summer, at night in the garden the plants and bushes would vibrate with sound and flashes of light, even though there was no wind and the curtains of the house were tightly drawn, leaving almost total blackness. My hostess Susanne told me that since she had moved into the countryside she had been aware of these nature essences and would leave out milk and honey for them, in keeping with the local custom.

To see the tiny moving spheres of energy, go to a fairy place on a winter's day late in the afternoon when the light is fading and half-close your eyes. You might like to make a wish.

Wish Magic

- Find out all you can about the magical character or characters associated with your chosen site.

- Take an offering with you to leave in a crevice – a silver coin, a special crystal, a tiny piece of jewellery, something that will sparkle and amplify the energies.

- When you reach the spot, formulate your wish in a few words. As you do so, the air bubbles of floating magical potential may instantly suggest new possibilities.

- Begin by invoking the blessing and help of the spirit of the place, the fairy queen, the King of the Elves, the guardian of the Otherworld entrance, a priestess or witch or the Lady of the Lake in her underwater palace. You are not summoning up spirits here, but focusing your energies on a symbolic form that has been given power over the centuries.

• Add a description of how you envisage the magical form so that you can clearly visualise the spirit of the place in front of you. For example, in a fairy glen you might invoke Oonagh, Queen of the Fairies, who was described by the Victorian Lady Wilde with 'golden hair sweeping to the ground, clad in silver gossamer glittering as if with diamonds, that were actually dew drops'.

• After naming your energy source, make your wish clearly and in a few words. Make it aloud if you are alone.

• Visualise the words being carried off into the twilight or darkness as though in bubbles, to swell as they join with other globes of energy and then to be transformed by the magical being with the wave of a hand or wand into the desired effect.

• At this point you may suddenly see your wish as an image in your mind. It may not be precisely what you asked for but will be what will fulfil your desire.

• You may experience a slight shimmering or feel suddenly excited and focused, hear words from the fairy form or experience a sense of a burden being lifted and a feeling that all will be well.

• Thank the fairy guardian of the place and leave your offering in a crevice or cast it into a pool or river.

• Linger a while absorbing the inspirational atmosphere and go back to the real world empowered and confident.

Even if you never *see* a fairy as such, you can feel them in woodlands, hear them as you sit on a hilltop; witness their swift movement within the foam of a waterfall or deep within a pool suddenly rippled on a windless day. You can also share the world of a creature of the night, either an animal close to the ground or a bird high in the night sky. Once we lose our sense of separation we can flow with these energies and share their freedom and wisdom.

10

The Otherworld
of Night

As well as night creatures and magical fairy folk, terrifying spectres are sometimes said to come out at night. Ghost stories tell of hideous phantoms who haunt the living. In fact the majority of ghosts who return after dark are benign. Many are deceased relatives who return to soothe a restless grandchild, or former residents who are attached to a dwelling or whose emotions and patterns are imprinted in certain rooms.

Other phantoms may appear in wild places, sometimes where strong human emotion is imprinted, perhaps on or close to the site of a former battlefield. Some ghosts who remain in places do so because they have not moved on to the next plane of existence, some because they cannot or do not want to.

Though ghosts may be seen during the daytime, they are associated primarily with the night, perhaps because as we tire, our conscious minds become less active in filtering out events we cannot explain.

Jim Cooke, an American paranormal investigator and a broadcaster for more than 30 years, told me:

I think that more paranormal activity is probably received at night and in the early morning hours. This is when most homes are very quiet, so events are more easily recognised. There is always a fair amount of psychic activity involved in a haunting. When people have communication with a ghost, it is either visual communication or telepathy – mind to mind. For this to happen most people would have to be in a relaxed state of mind. Naturally, most people are relaxed at night-time.

The Wise Ancestors

In traditional cultures from China and Japan to Africa, a deceased relation is still revered and regarded as part of the family or tribe. In Westernised industrial society in contrast, people can become very frightened of the idea of ancestors returning in spirit form. However, in my own research into this field I have been given countless examples of how a deceased relation has come back to comfort, advise or even save the life of a family member. Love seems to overcome even death.

Dawn, a retired restaurant owner, recently lost her mother and sister to cancer. She was distressed not only by their loss but because her sister had died before they had sorted out her mother's financial affairs. As a result there were problems that were causing family stress.

She described how she was sitting on her bed when suddenly rays of purple light radiated from the overhead lamp and her mother walked in. She sat next to Dawn on the bed and held her, telling her that she loved her and had not meant the problems to occur but that everything would be fine. Dawn said her mother felt warm, quite solid and three-dimensional, but she was afraid to move in case she disappeared. In fact she left as she had come, through the door.

Such experiences are intensely comforting and have happened to so many sensible rational people that they cannot be dismissed as imagination or wishful thinking.

However, some equally loving families do not have contact and there is no reason that can be given. Some people are happy to live with the memories and to work through grief in their own way. Others seek some tangible contact. For those seeking contact with a beloved relation, graveyards are not the place to look. Nor is visiting a medium the right way for everyone to make what may be a private statement of love and grief, though some people do find genuine mediums very helpful.

The following method is one that has been helpful to a number of people who have needed to have some tangible contact with a person who has died.

Contacting a Deceased Family Member

- As the Sun is setting, sit in the growing twilight in front of a large mirror, if possible one used by the deceased family member.

- Light two small pink and two small green candles for love and reconciliation and let the light reflect in the mirror and serve as illumination for the room.

- You are not calling up a spirit, nor should you try, but are recreating and recalling the love of someone close. If the experience feels wrong, stop.

- Ask that your special angel or guardian spirit protect you as you work and that you will work only for the highest good.

- Hold an item of clothing or a treasured possession that belonged to the person, perhaps a scarf, a ring or a well-loved book. Alternatively, choose a gift they made to you.

- Looking into the glass, project from your mind's eye the image of the deceased person, focusing on their smile and eyes filled with love and gentleness.

- For some people a faint image does appear in the glass, while for others the person remains within the mind, enhanced by the reflective beams from the mirror.

- Speak soft words of love, reconciliation or regret and visualise within the mirror the person looking back at you in acceptance and with approval. This can be especially helpful if you were not able to say goodbye or the person deteriorated physically or mentally with an illness, making the death particularly sad.

- You may notice that the person in the vision looks well, strong and younger than when you last saw them.

- You may also feel a gentle breeze, a soft sigh, perfume or a particular fragrance associated with your loved one, a gossamer-light touch in your hair or on your shoulder or just an incredible sense of peace and of being loved.

• Recreate in your mind a shared moment of pleasure, a happy outing or holiday, a joke, a small triumph or a meaningful and positive conversation. You may hear with your inner ear the now departed voice echoing familiar words or soft laughter.

• When you are ready, say goodbye and wish the person, God or Goddess speed. It is important you do not try to use love to hold the person back. They may come to you in a dream or present a sign if you are patient.

Some loved ones make contact quickly. Others return after months or even years. For some people there is never direct contact, rather a sense of being cherished, like sitting in a room reading with someone whose connection you can sense, although no words or glances are exchanged.

Do not try to use Ouija boards or séances to call up relations. These are dangerous, psychologically as well as in deeper ways. If you feel you would like help, contact a reputable medium through a local Spiritualist church or a spiritual healer from an accredited organisation.

Ghosts and Natural Phenomena

A particular site may be the scene of ghostly visitations over a period of hundreds of years. As mentioned earlier, this may be because people have tried to explain the powers they feel in such a sacred place. However, it may also be that because the place has such powerful earth energies ghosts can use them to manifest in earthly form. The explanations are not mutually exclusive.

Though ghostly phenomena are usually reported at night, some sightings take place during the day in dark forest places and deep misty lakes. In New Zealand there are a number of ghostly Maori canoe tales. For example, the author and paranormal researcher Dorothy O'Donnell of Christchurch describes a phantom Maori who rows across Lake Tajawere just before the volcano close by erupts. Maori legends sometimes describe the journey to the Afterworld as being by canoe.

Other ghosts appear at a regular time as evening shadows fall and are accepted by locals as part of the landscape. In 1839 Abraham Elder, a historian and folklorist, described in his book *Tales and Legends of the Isle of Wight* a tall man dressed in black who at night would take a seat on the passenger ferry that crossed from St Helens to Bembridge. He was seen by the ferryman and by a number of passengers, but would disappear midway across the water. The ferry crossing is close to one of the major ley or psychic energy lines on the Isle of Wight, a small island off the south coast of England which is my home.

Small islands have more than their fair share of ghosts because the energies of sea, sky and earth are concentrated in a confined area, which seems to energise paranormal essences.

As you work with the night energies, you will become aware of presences and psychic atmospheres that others may miss.

Earth Lights

Sometimes paranormal energies may manifest not as figures but as lights hovering over a wild location at night. These 'earth lights' may appear over centuries in the same place. Often these are areas of high energy, for example where ley lines cross.

Earth lights are found in many parts of the world. They have been reported hovering over ancient stones, especially at the old seasonal festivals. At Avebury Ring in the UK, for centuries they have been perceived as small luminous figures dancing around the stones just above the ground, especially on May Eve.

Earth lights have even been linked to alien encounters, for example at Hessdalen valley 70 miles (112 km) south-east of Trondheim in Norway. White and yellow spheres and also bullet and inverted fir-tree-shaped lights were first seen in the area in November 1981. These phenomena continued and after hundreds of reports from locals, Norwegian and Swedish UFO groups continuously monitored the area for just over a month beginning on 21 January 1984. During this period, photographs of the lights were obtained and the lights seemed to read the thoughts of the investigators and respond to them.

Invariably you will find a higher than average number of ghost sightings in the areas where earth lights and other inexplicable psychic phenomena such as crop circles occur. Crop circles are flattened circles of corn, often in intricate patterns, many of which appear suddenly during the night without any evidence of human intervention.

The Brown Mountain Earth Lights

Jason Boone is an American psychic researcher. He told me about the lights of Brown Mountain in the foothills of the Blue Ridge Parkway, which is just outside Morganton, North Carolina, in Burke County. According to official information the lights are visible between sunset and sunrise, especially between 10 p.m. and 2 a.m. and are most prevalent in September and October. Jason told me:

> *The mountain is for the most part uninhabited and people usually stay off it ... The lights themselves have been seen since way back during the days of the Native Americans. Scientists have stated that the cause could be sulphur or other swamp gases that ignite once they reach the Earth's surface. This isn't so, because none of the gases are found in this area and there are no swamps in the region of Brown Mountain.*
>
> *Others say that the lights are reflections off the Moon. However, they still occur when there is no moonlight at all. Another explanation is that the lights are cars or trains that pass through the mountain. But the lights were seen before transport and electricity came to the area. What is more, in 1916 a great flood that swept through the Catawba Valley knocked out the railroad bridges, roads and power lines for more than a week, yet the lights still appeared.*
>
> *Some people believe that the mountains are haunted by ghosts, fairies and will o' the wisps. A few locals insist that the lights are linked with the sightings of what is known as the woolly booger, a headless bear that has been sighted on the mountain on occasions.*

As Jason says, the lights are part of the local Native American tradition and their legends first spoke of them around 1200, when a battle was fought near the mountain between the Cherokee and Catawba. The Cherokee say that the lights are the Indian women still searching for their lost husbands and lovers.

The lights were first reported officially by the German engineer Geraud de Brahm, the first outsider to reach the area in 1771. They vary in intensity and appearance from glowing balls of fire to skyrockets and whirling pinwheels of light.

Ghostly candidates for the paranormal activity include a planter who became lost in the mountains while hunting and whose devoted slave searched for him night after night with a lantern. Both perished, but it is said that the slave still looks for his master with his lantern. Another possible source of paranormal energy is a woman who was murdered by her husband in 1850. Her body was found on the mountain many years later.

Tunnel Ghosts

Quiet dark places such as old canals or railway tunnels are another favourite location for ghosts, especially tunnels that have been abandoned or are rarely used. Usually there is an identifiable ghost who died in tragic or inexplicable circumstances in the tunnel. Canal and railway tunnels seem to attract such hauntings, perhaps because the energies are concentrated in the enclosed dark place like psychic echoes.

One of the most fascinating tunnels is Redbank Range Railway Tunnel, known as Picton Tunnel, in New South Wales, Australia. It was opened in February 1867 and was eventually closed to trains in 1919. During the Second World War it was used to store ammunition and other military supplies. The resident ghost is Emily Bollard who was killed in the centre of the tunnel in 1916. It has never been established whether this was suicide or an accident.

Rowena of the New South Wales Castle of Spirits organisation explained:

The apparition of Emily has been seen on quite a few separate occasions. She appears usually as a white flowing figure of a woman with no face. She, or another ghost, has also appeared as a black shadow that is regularly seen on the walls and throughout the tunnel and has appeared in front of a tour member while standing in the dark of the tunnel.

On occasions black shadows have been viewed rapidly moving up the entire length of the tunnel towards a tour group. People have reported white lights hovering above people's heads, figures appearing in front and behind in the blackness, ghostly children and strange electrical appearances travelling down the tunnel. Some people have gone in there late at night with a group of friends and still refuse to speak about what happened to them in there.

Urban Ghosts

Even in towns with modern shopping precincts and new developments you may find corners of history with ghosts. Areas where there have been major historical events, a battle or a major plague outbreak, are natural ghost spots. In towns such as Gettysburg, where many young soldiers perished in the bloody battles of July 1863, almost every house has a paranormal story.

The cellars, dusty attics and basements of old buildings can all house ghosts, especially if they were once part of far older properties whose ghosts still linger. Pauline now lives in Australia but she grew up in Scotland and her grandmother worked near what is now one of the favourite ghosts walks in Edinburgh. She gave her account in the Scottish Society for Psychical Research's journal:

From the age of four I often went in the evenings to help my granny who worked as a cleaner in the Royal Bank in Tron Square in Edinburgh.

The Bank itself was the epitome of old-world magnificence and craftsmanship with beautifully polished counters, ornate plasterwork on the ceiling and marble flooring. The cellars, however, were a different story. They were reached down plain stone stairs and along a wide barren passageway and were massive and cavern-like. Off this main corridor was another corridor of which, for as long as I can remember, I had a dread.

Granny's niece, Kathleen, was ten years old and one night decided to help Granny with us. I was five years old and a bit scared of this big girl. As the night wore on and Kathleen and I went down to the cellar to empty waste paper bins into a big sack, we seemed to be getting on fine.

'Do you want to see what's along this corridor?' she asked me.

Off I trotted, happy that Kathleen could reach the light switch that I could not. At the end of the long passage a huge door blocked the way. Kathleen found a key for the padlock. Very soon we were inside what I discovered was the coal cellar. I was intrigued by this and remembered Granny telling me that the coalman came every Thursday and that she got the place ready for each new lot of coal.

What I was not ready for was the door closing with a slam and the light outside being turned off, leaving me standing in complete darkness, unable to move with fright. I ran to the door, falling over coal on the way, screaming and banging on the door and crying at the same time.

What I heard was something quite different. It was sniffling and weeping, coming from the huge high coal area. I turned round slowly, staring at what was behind me. Paralysed with fear and not knowing what to do, I beheld a crowd of people sitting on the coal, the stark black only highlighting the pale outlines in dim white. Mothers with babies, men and women holding each other in pain and fear and lots of old people. All came towards me as if trying to tell me something. I felt them say, 'Don't be afraid. Do not cry.'

But that only made me worse. Within a few moments they were right beside me, reaching out as if to comfort me. I was petrified. Then after what seemed an eternity, the light in the corridor went on.

Granny opened the great door and I was free, crying and sobbing and telling her what I had seen. She said: 'They'll no' harm you, lassie, they're just poor souls trying to help you.'

Not until the late 1970s did it become known that Edinburgh's Royal Mile was built directly on an older city and that plague had wiped out many of the previous inhabitants. Ghost tours are conducted around the waxworks on the High Street, just beside the Bank's cellars. I can sympathise now with those poor souls, as Granny called them, to whom she talked every Thursday before the coalman came.

Ghosts vs Psychic Imprints

So what is it we see or experience when we visit such places? Jim Cooke, the American paranormal researcher, comments that some ghosts that people see may not really be ghosts at all:

There is a very good chance that an apparition is an image that was somehow implanted in the location and repeats itself over and over again, like videotape. This type of apparition tends to happen in locations that have higher that normal magnetic fields or energies present. If conditions are right, a person who is sensitive enough and is in a relaxed state of mind will be able to see this event.

Some ghosts do speak to us, however, and it is only when they suddenly disappear into thin air that we realise we were talking to a phantom. Helena, who lives in Stockholm, was camping on one of the many uninhabited wooded islands in a remote part of the region. She told me:

My boyfriend Christer and I moored up late in the evening while it was still light and made our camp. Ours was the only boat and we were moored on the only possible landing site. Christer set up his fishing rods and I walked off in the remaining light into the woods to search for a rare night bird whose call I had heard as we moored.

I stayed in the woods longer than I had intended and darkness was falling fast. I lost my bearings and was about to yell for Christer when I saw an oldish woman in a brown dress down to her ankles, who seemed to be gathering berries. She smiled and spoke in Swedish but with a heavy accent and dialect I did not recognise. Her face was quite scarred with what looked like chickenpox marks. She said: 'Your boat is back that way.' She led me for a short way until I was back on the main path. Then she disappeared quite literally in front of my eyes, as if she dissolved into darkness.

I ran back and Christer thought I was joking. But at my insistence he searched the wooded area but found no one. I stayed welded to his side all night and in the morning again we searched every inch of those woods. But there was no woman, no shelter and no provisions.

When we went home, I tried to find out about the island but could discover nothing. I wondered if the woman had caught smallpox and had been isolated there in some earlier age. I do not know.

Encountering Ghosts

You might like to track down some ghosts for yourself. Work at night, in the evening or early morning or in a naturally dark place on a winter's day with poor physical visibility. This helps the dimensions to merge and your psychic senses to take priority.

Begin your ghost watching in an area where there are reported paranormal events such as earth lights or crop circles. Alternatively, you might choose a place that is endowed with strong emotion, for example former battlefields such as Gettysburg in America or Culloden in Scotland, which seem to reveal their ghosts even to people who find it difficult initially to tune in to paranormal power spots.

For more peaceful ghosts you might decide to visit a ruined abbey or an old castle on a late winter's afternoon or in the early morning on one of those days when it never gets fully light. Some ruins you can walk around at night. Here you can tune in to the essences of monks and nuns who may have etched deep contentment on every stone, or of castle servants who followed the same routine all their lives in a place that may have been their only home from late childhood.

Workplaces or industrial museums where artefacts and buildings have been recreated using the original materials also hold their ghosts. The workshops may have high or barred windows and be dimly lit, if at all, by gaslight. Visit on dark afternoons just before closing time.

Seek out also areas of deep forest, caves, cellars, canal towpaths with dark tunnels, disused railway tunnels and original districts of old towns to which ghost legends are attached. Even if there is hype, there was usually an original genuine sighting that gave the place its reputation.

Don't shun ghost tours around towns or to haunted houses. I used to until I realised what a valuable store of information I was missing. You may not see any ghosts, but you can learn the specific places where phantoms have been seen, hear stories of their characters and pick up atmospheres that will give you a good start to your own private and more leisurely exploration.

The old festivals are times when the dimensions move closer together. The most powerful are Halloween, the beginning of the Celtic New Year, when the dead mingle with the living; the more modern New Year's Day, before dawn; and May Eve, the beginning of the Celtic summer. The Summer Solstice around 21 June and the Midwinter Solstice around 21 December also have energies of change that can stir up paranormal activity. All of these times were popular for fairy sightings.

Dusk, dawn and midnight are also powerful transition points. The Celtic year began at sunset. The dark of the Moon (before it is visible in the sky) is also good for ghost sightings.

Beginning Ghost Hunting

- Before you begin your ghost hunt, protect yourself psychically from free-floating energies. Carry a small crystal of the kind you use for your focal altar crystal and breathe in the energies of this smaller but no less potent version before attempting your search for ghosts. Also, ask for the protection of your special angel or night guardian.

- You may also pass one of your protective crystals through the smoke of a pine or sandalwood incense stick and the light of a purple candle, asking that you may be protected as you work. Carry the crystal with you.

- Find out about the history and legends of your chosen location and walk around in daylight to absorb the atmosphere.

- Spend this time looking for hints of the past, engravings over buildings, unusual street names, a building from an earlier period than those around it, original cobbles or wrought iron work in an alleyway.

Using Psychometry on a Ghost Hunt

As I said earlier, we have minor chakras or energy centres in the soles of our feet and palms of our hands. We can absorb a great deal of psychic information through these energy centres that can enable us to tune in to otherworldly energies quite spontaneously.

- As it gets dark or late on a winter's afternoon, make contact through your hands and feet with any old stones, bricks or artefacts or with the trees in a forest. If you are on sand or grass and it is not too cold, walk barefoot. You may see images of past times or get impressions that may suggest a certain character to you.

- Take your time and allow these impressions to build up quite spontaneously. You may hear words or singing, the cries of market vendors or the peal of church bells in your head, or receive feelings of elation, peace, love or unhappiness.

- You may be picking up the emotions of the people who once walked these paths, perhaps a particular person with whom you share spiritual kinship across the ages. This may not be the ghost of local legend but another person who is equally interesting.

- If you do not seem to be focusing on a particular person from the past, allow your mind to create a whole scene from the past of the place you are in. Continue to keep physical contact with the place with your hands or feet, but focus in your mind on one figure in the scene, someone to whom you are instinctively drawn. As if turning a lens in your mind, bring them into focus. This is your ghost.

- Alternatively, ask the spirits of the place if you may try to catch a glimpse of them. If the answer is negative in your mind or you feel a slight jaggedness, do not intrude. The time is not right.

- If the answer is positive, focus on a dark corner of the present physical scene and using a small torch flash the light on and off very fast two or three times. You may, if you are lucky, have a momentary image of a ghost framed in their silvery aura, the glow around the outline of a phantom.

- Now allow your mind's vision to take over. Gaze into the darkness and move inwards from where you perceived the ghost aura. Close your eyes if necessary and visualise the ghost's frame.

- Open your eyes and you may see the phantom clothed in a garment of their period. It would seem that a spirit body projects an image of themselves as they were when alive.

- Many ghosts do seem unaware of our presence. However, if the phantom does smile or speak, then you can smile and answer. Some ghosts have a message, perhaps concerning their death or a significant event in their lives that was unresolved. If so, listen, thank the ghost for the message and move away. It takes an experienced medium to deal with spirit rescue and it is very dangerous to try to interfere in affairs of another age or dimension. Many encounters are much more subtle, though, and you may be rewarded by a smell of a particular flower or spice, a song or the sound of church bells carried across the ages. Whatever you are offered in the way of paranormal experience, take it with gratitude.

- Whether or not the ghost interacts with you, end the encounter with a blessing such as 'Go in peace, friend.' Walk away and do not look back.

• Go home and offer a prayer for the peace of your phantom, but do not return to the same place. Relationships across the dimensions, even if possible, are not advisable.

If you sensed a troubled soul you might like to ask your special night guardian or angel to protect the soul and guide them to their rest.

If you ever feel afraid or have a sense that all is not well during a ghost encounter, leave the place immediately, offering a prayer for peace for all who remain there. The spirits will not follow you. But psychic work, especially if a place has sad associations, can be draining.

After any ghost hunting, have a bath with rose or lavender essential oil and sleep with a dark banded or moss agate or jade under your pillow.

Dealing with Ghosts

As you become more psychically aware you may see ghosts quite spontaneously and start to see images of people you do not know in your mind just before you sleep. This may be the beginning of the evolution of mediumship abilities. If you do not want to develop them, view the images like pictures on a television screen and switch them off by drawing down a dark velvet screen from the crown of your head to your heart.

If you do want to learn to control and use your powers, talk to the president of your local Spiritualist church or to someone at a healing federation, as evolving mediumship and healing abilities often emerge together.

Earlier I suggested ways of dealing with unhappy ghosts in your home and when it is best to seek advice from a priest or medium (*see page 38*). With ghosts you meet in other settings, if you sense unhappiness or malevolent energies, leave. Do not attempt spirit rescue or sending ghosts into the light. The place you are in may have collected a number of entities, and even experienced mediums would need to work as a group and with much protection. If you feel afraid, surround yourself with visualised light, make a blessing and move on.

My own favourite ghost experience was when my middle son Jack was a few months old. The family was staying in Brittany and we had gone to the ruined château at Suscinio near Vannes. I was sitting in a window recess in an empty room when suddenly I was aware of a fire blazing in the hearth and a woman in red feeding her baby in a carved chair opposite. It was as if glass or a mist separated us but I was aware she could see me and we were just two women sitting companionably with our babies. Then I heard the calls of the older children, and as they entered there was a gust of wind and the woman and the fire were gone. For me that is the essence of ghost experiences – nothing dramatic, but two people momentarily meeting across the centuries and sharing a smile.

In the final chapter we will return to the light, empowered by our positive experiences of the night.

11

Returning to the Light

Empowered by our dreams and night rituals, protected by Archangels, guided by the stars, we rode on our shamanic journeys on the back of our chosen night steed. We sat in our special night place mediating, praying, creating rituals or asking for healing and help.

As the night fades, dawn brings the day we anticipated or perhaps dreaded. Every dawn is a triumph of light, a re-enactment of Creation itself as light is born of darkness. Each day we can generate new energies, new beginnings, rekindle the spark of inner creativity and resilience that sometimes may be all we have in our favour.

We can use the precious moments of transition between day and night to bring the dreams, desires and petitions we empowered with night magic to fulfilment in the everyday world. For the rising power of the Sun illuminates and gives life to the thought forms we wove and nurtured on the dark planes when anything seemed possible.

Working with the Dawn

Dawn varies each day. Its precise time can be found in a diary or the weather section of a newspaper. Its energies too vary, according to the weather, the time of year and the location – fiery orange, pink and red, clear white light or misty pearl, fierce or gentle, eager or reluctant to disturb the encompassing dark . . .

Dawn is associated with the East and is represented in ritual by facing East. However, since the Sun only rises in the true East (and sets in the West) on the Equinoxes, because of the tilt of the Earth, you may wish to work with its actual position in the sky as it breaks through.

A Dawn Ritual

The power of the first light of morning rising from darkness is akin to the power of a plane taking off from the tarmac. Healing rituals at many sacred wells were timed to finish just as dawn broke to take advantage of the energy of the transition.

- Work outdoors if at all possible. If not, go as high as you can in your house in a room facing approximately East and set a table with a white cloth near the window.

- Outdoors spread a white cloth on the ground to use as an altar.

- Just before dawn take a crystal bowl of pure water and set it on the cloth.

- Hold a clear pointed quartz crystal in your power hand and hold a lighted Sun incense such as frankincense, bay or rosemary in your other hand.

- In an arc over the crystal use the smoke to write in the night air a wish, a desire, the name of someone you love or even that of someone you hate, though you know the bad feelings are hurting you. By writing in smoke you are sending your wish, your love or your bad feelings into the cosmos. Here they will be transformed into light energy and so amplified in the case of positive thoughts or dissipated if they were dark or sad.

- Return the incense to a holder and raise the bowl in the darkness.

- Whisper or repeat in your mind the empowerment or banishment you wrote in the darkness and add: 'May the light of fulfilment/healing rise from the dark waters and the dark skies. Blessings be.'

- Replace the bowl and wait as light returns, not visualising anything or trying to focus on your wish.

- The dawn chorus of birds, even in a town, will help you to merge with the awakening energies.

- Allow yourself by gentle breathing to become the last vestiges of night, to experience the stirring of light within you as it is rippling in the air, illuminating the fibres of the darkness.

- When there is light, hold your crystal over the bowl and wait for it to fill with light. It may seem heavier. Allow the light to fill you also, without making any conscious effort to absorb it.

- When the crystal is full to overflowing and you can feel the life force bubbling likewise within you, plunge the crystal into the water so that drops splash on your face, saying: 'Darkness to light, day reborn, I greet the promise of the morning with my own renewed flame of hope.'

- Shake the crystal dry and place it in a purse or pouch to carry with you during the day.

- In the evening you can set the crystal on your night altar. Leave it outdoors overnight to catch the first rays of dawn whenever you need renewed confidence and energy.

- Filter your dawn water into a clear bottle and use some in your morning bath. You can also add your water to drinks, splash it on your pulse points when you are exhausted and give it to wilting plants.

- Mix the water with your full Moon water for a perfect balance of energy when you feel out of sorts with yourself and life. Make tea or coffee with the water or add it to cold drinks to bring you harmony. Use it also in refreshments for difficult colleagues or critical relations to soften their words. Add a few drops to the water bowl of hyperactive animals or to the baths of anxious children or stressed teenagers. Sprinkle it on the doorstep to make homecomings tranquil.

The Spring Equinox

Just as dawn marks the transition between night and day, so the Spring Equinox around 21 March heralds the beginning of the light half of the year when day becomes longer than night. In the Celtic tradition it started with the previous sunset, when the young god of light defeated his brother the god of darkness.

The Christian festival of Easter celebrates the resurrection of Christ and has absorbed all the original customs of the Equinox – the painted eggs, the Easter hare, sacred to Ostara, Viking goddess of spring, and even the hot cross buns that were originally Equinox cakes. These were marked with the old astrological sign for the Earth and the Earth Mother, a diagonal equal-armed cross, and so when people ate them they absorbed the magic of the rising light. The Sun danced in the waters at dawn on this most magical day.

A Spring Equinox Ritual

You can celebrate the Equinox either on the actual date in March or at Easter.

Because we have been working with the energies of the night, begin just before dawn, the most powerful transition point of the year.

You can use the festival for really important changes or surges of new life – everything from conceiving a baby to launching a new career, especially if there have been delays in getting your venture started or if it has not been working out. You can also seek new love or an infusion of energy and optimism.

- If possible, work out of doors if it is warm enough or in an upper room facing East.

- Before dawn, light yellow and bright green candles and decorate eggs that you have boiled in pastel natural food-colouring water with spirals, flowers and leaves in darker shades. This follows the old tradition of painting and offering the first eggs of the season to the shrine of the goddess of spring. If it is windy you can use glass holders to shelter your candles.

- Place the eggs in a small basket decorated with the first leaves and flowers of spring or, if you live in a warmer or colder climate, the flowers that bloom at this time. Traditional Spring Equinox flowers include celandine, cinquefoil, crocus, daffodils, honeysuckle, primroses and violets.

• Add to the basket one or two tiny Equinox crystals such as citrine, the strengthening stone, yellow beryl, the energiser, or a yellow rutilated quartz with streaks of gold, the regenerator.

• Finally scatter a few seeds in the basket, naming a new beginning or hope for the future with each one.

• Set your finished basket on a green or yellow cloth on either the ground or the table and watch for the first light, allowing visions of your fulfilled dreams to flow.

• As the first light breaks through, blow out your candles, saying: 'Darkness to light, night to morn, winter to spring, life reborn.'

• Using the flowers and the seeds, make nine concentric circles, moving outwards from the basket (or surround it with nine circles), reciting the traditional rhyme associated with spring cleaning: 'One for joy, two for gladness, three and four to banish sadness, five and six flee useless anger, seven, eight, nine, linger no longer. Nine, eight, seven, six, five, four, three, two, one, darker days now be gone.'

• When it is fully light, add more flowers and leaves to the basket, if possible some you have gathered from your garden or from plants you have grown.

• Give the basket to someone to whom it will bring pleasure as your offering to the energies of the spring.

Bringing the Shadow Self into the Light

We have worked in a number of places in the book with our shadow self and know that like the night it is a repository of hidden talents and energies. So as we return to the light, the shadow self also will feel free to play in the sunshine and no longer lurk in the shadows, waiting for nightfall.

Walking with Your Shadow into the Light

- The early morning is an excellent time for working with your physical shadow, which is a manifestation of your spirit shadow.

- Begin in a dark place and walk in clear early morning sunlight so that your shadow can emerge from its sanctuary. Experiment with different Sun angles so that your shadow walks beside you, occasionally darting back into the shade until you are ready to bring it in front of you.

- Greet your shadow as you would your dearest friend and it will offer you gifts from the store of talents with which you came into the world. There may be one area of your life that you know needs additional resources or you may suddenly become aware of a new opportunity.

- Hold out your hand to accept the gift and touch your heart to accept it within. Thank your shadow.

- If you feel ready, extend your hand again to your shadow. Ask that some hidden sorrow, a sad memory or disappointment you have repressed, perhaps for years, may be dispersed in the light of day.

- Be very gentle with yourself and your shadow, as you may momentarily relive emotions you have long buried.

- Now release your hand and toss the dark matter towards the Sun, where it will be absorbed in a sunbeam.

- Before leaving your shadow, play as you did when a child – lifting one leg, trying to outrun your shadow, waving, clapping, dancing.

- When you are ready, embrace your shadow. Return to the darker area and leave your physical shadow. However, you know that this very precious part of yourself is within.

Whenever you need to draw on your store of abilities or are ready to shed another burden from the past, your shadow will be waiting in the early morning. You need only call and it will emerge from the shadows to walk with you into the light.

Loving the Night

Night is a very special time for ritual and for exploring the hidden aspects of our nature that hold so much potential and power. With its dark places and silence, night offers sanctuary against the harsh light and noise of the modern world and enables us to hear our own inner voice and see visions on the dark screen of our inner eye. In sleep, too, our psychic selves can find freedom and can move beyond the limitations of time and space into infinity.

Each person develops unique gifts by working with the night. These might include releasing fears and being calm inside and less subject to the pressures of everyday problems. Certainly you will be wiser, more intuitive and connected with the ebbs and flows of your own energies, and these will gradually move closer to those of the natural cycles of nature.

This new inner strength and serenity will have effects in the outer world, making you healthier and more open to attracting love and good fortune, because your psychic energy field is no longer clogged by doubts and low self-esteem. You will even be more decisive and more tuned in to daily life because you have learned to trust your own decision-making. The person who walks with harmony through the night can tread the daytime paths with equal certainty.

If we learn to love Mother Night she will lull us in her womb and share with us the secrets of her treasure box of stars. She will introduce us to her creatures that live in the shadows and if we can learn to be still and silent we may see fleetingly the magical essences that dance in the moonlight and make their homes deep in the hollow hills and dark forests.

Darkness is the seamless cloak that spans the dimensions, offering assurance that death is not the end, allowing us to learn from past worlds and glimpse future possibilities.

As I finish this book, the Moon is rising over the caravan where I work, though it is still not quite dark. Already the night creatures are scurrying in the grass, the rabbits peering from their holes until it is safe to come out and eat my newly planted herbs.

Reaching my home on the other side of the island, I see the Moon high in the sky and the stars scattered in a glittering pathway. My ancestors saw the same night wonders. My descendants will likewise look up at the stars, which will hardly have changed over hundreds of years.

I no longer fear the darkness. I know that summer will follow winter, day follow night. As I pause outside the lighted window of my house, watching my teenagers sprawled in their heap of happiness and unwashed dishes, I wonder if one day my ghost may likewise see my great-grandchildren through lighted windows, as I know my late mother watches over our family.

As you sit by your night altar or in your night place, you join with people all over the world and in other ages who have celebrated the powers of the night and used them for healing, for protection and for power.

Darkness was the first state before Creation. 'Who will walk into the darkness with me?' is the cry of the Crone goddess. Look into her face. She has the loving eyes of your wise grandmother. If you take her hand and walk with faith you will never stumble or be lost, even in the darkest and loneliest night.

May your dreams be wonderful and their realisation even better.

Cassandra
23 April, 2002

Appendix I

Dream Symbolism

These are some of the most common dream meanings and can form the basis for your own more extensive list. You can record them in your Book of Shadows along with your scrying symbols, which will be very similar.

Every dream meaning can have positive or negative significance according to the emotions experienced in the dream. Even negative dreams can offer solutions to problems and suggest new ways forward.

Accident Advance warning from your subconscious of potential hazards or unacknowledged worries.

Angel Awareness of a spirit helper; emergence of personal spiritual awareness.

Bees Money coming or unexpected communication on family matters; if stung, fear of a sudden attack, perhaps from a matriarchal figure.

Birds Messengers; a desire for increased freedom and travel or unacknowledged personal ambitions; if caged, a warning of being trapped by a situation.

Blindness/complete darkness Stepping into the unknown, facing and overcoming fears of mortality and separateness; if afraid or in danger in the darkness, vulnerability and fear of physical or emotional attack, or of dependency.

Bride/groom/weddings If your wedding, desire for a closer relationship and for assurance that the relationship will last; if a different bride or groom from your current partner, problems in the current relationship need resolving; if you are a guest, being sidelined at work or in a relationship.

Bull Male power, sexuality and courage; the determination to overcome all obstacles; unacknowledged anger or suppressed illicit passion.

Butterfly Rebirth and regeneration; the need to enjoy present happiness without demanding permanence; rebirth of hope and trust; if trapped, torn or dying, trying to hold on to a rapidly changing situation or unresolved loss or grief.

Cancer Not a prediction, but a powerful indication of bitterness, resentment or obsession; fears about health and mortality.

Cats Desire for independence; an untamed instinctive spirit; undeveloped psychic powers; if fierce, fear of others' hidden spite or your own jealous or resentful feelings bursting out.

Cave Archetypal symbol of the womb; conception, pregnancy and birth of both ideas and a child; if unwilling to leave the cave, a need to be mothered; if trapped in a cave, being stifled by a mothering situation or fear of emotional independence.

Chase/escape The impetus to pursue desires and ambitions; being chased, unwelcome responsibilities or overwhelming demands; if chasing but not catching a desired person or object, unrealistic expectations or not really wanting it after all.

Children If you want children, a preview of a future as a parent; if you are the child, a desire to return to the past, possibly for nurturing; if wounded, old emotional scars have not healed; if your own children are involved in a disaster, an expression of your buried anxieties for their safety or their own possible fears about life.

City The desire for a more stimulating environment, either physically or intellectually, especially if the city is abroad or unfamiliar; if lost in a city or living in a derelict area, feelings of isolation or being out of your depth in a potentially hostile situation.

Coffin/death/funeral Laying to rest redundant situations or relationships, guilt or fears; avoiding a natural ending; worries about serious illness and mortality or redundancy.

Contamination/infectious disease A need to clear out negative influences; if contaminated food or water supply or an infectious disease, fears of being influenced negatively by others or losing control of your own destiny.

Demons/the Devil A desire to break free of external prohibitions and to express your sexuality and power; if being harmed or entrapped by the demons, hostile feelings and fears, especially your own, are overwhelming because you are trying to deny them.

Dogs Fidelity and loyal friendship, possibly unrecognised; an indication that you should follow your instincts; if ferocious, a fear of hostility, especially your own uncontrolled anger and aggression.

Dragons Power, sexuality, hidden talents that need expression; if fire-breathing, destructive urges or sexual frustration or a bullying superior at work or an over-critical lover.

Drowning Initiation into a new stage of awareness; a major change; fears of being overwhelmed by an inability to cope, though presenting a cheerful face to the world; if a family member is drowning, fear that you cannot protect them from the dangers of the world.

Earthquake A complete shake-up of old ideas, a new order emerging from the old; fear of dramatic change not of your own making; deep insecurity about a relationship, job or finances.

Failure Never a warning of failure, but may show an area where apparent success might not bring happiness; if failing an examination or interview, general fears of not living up to the expectations of others.

Falling Letting go of inhibitions, especially sexually, and opening up to new experiences; fear of losing security and control and facing possible pain or loss.

Father Desire for wise counsel and guidance, for material security or personal striving for success; if forbidding, a negative past voice which still unconsciously acts as a brake on joy and initiative.

Fighting/armies/war Taking action against injustice or stagnation; unresolved aggression; fear of aggression and conflict; a war can suggest a long struggle.

Floating Freedom from restrictions and total inner harmony; possible out-of-body travel; potential sexual bliss; if floating through total emptiness, a sense of isolation and purposelessness.

Floods/tidal waves Washing away what is redundant or destructive; a sudden surge of inspiration or understanding; initiation into a new stage of awareness, sexual release or surging passion; if trapped or drowning, being overwhelmed by repressed emotions or actual responsibilities and problems.

Flying Like floating, associated with astral travel, lucid dreaming and sexual ecstasy; if piloting or flying in a plane, widening opportunities, the former through taking control of personal destiny; if afraid of flying, a terror of losing control emotionally or sexually.

Food If enjoying a feast or good food, a sensual uninhibited nature and the ability to express pleasure; if grossly fat or feeling ashamed or sick when you eat, emotional issues related to food and a dissatisfaction with your body.

Forest/jungle Your untamed nature and natural instincts; an indication you should take a risk; if lost or pursued in a jungle or dark forest, turbulent emotions that threaten to surface or a reluctance to commit emotionally or sexually.

Garden If well tended, controlled creativity through patient application and the translation of inspiration into practical plans; if barren or untended, a neglect of spiritual and emotional growth in favour of others' needs.

Ghost A deceased relation with a message of comfort, reconciliation or advice; if a stranger, information not accessible to the conscious mind; if frightening or malevolent, unresolved and frightening issues in the real world.

Giant A huge ambition or undertaking; if friendly, help in advancing important projects; if terrifying, fear about major issues or hostility from people who seem intimidating or being overwhelmed by insurmountable problems.

Gift If a prize given by someone famous, you may be seeking recognition of input and promotion; if you are giving the gift, you are seeking love and approval from the recipient; if you are disappointed by a gift or do not receive one when you are expecting it, you may be giving too much to others or not expressing your own needs clearly enough.

Grandmother/wise woman/witch Wisdom, compassion and guidance from deep within your psyche; if malevolent, fear of death, old age and ugliness, both inner and outer.

Gypsy Desire to travel and to be free of unnecessary restrictions; restlessness and alienation, especially in a domestic situation; an older gypsy woman may be a guide, perhaps of your emerging divinatory skills or wisdom of the countryside and love.

Hill/mountain If climbing one effortlessly and/or reaching the top, success and fulfilment within reach; if barren or one where the peak gets further away the higher you climb, frustration, slow progress and obstacles.

Holidays Wider horizons, actual travel; if happy, a pleasant trip; if unhappy, you may feel guilty about leaving responsibilities behind; if you do not want the holiday to end or dream of the last day, your life may have become unduly burdensome.

Home If a childhood home or an idealised house, a reminder of the security you once had and would like again or a growing desire for a secure base and maybe a family; if dirty and cluttered, there is much you wish to discard or radically change in your home life.

Horse A desire for movement, either in the outer or inner world, or for a deep love commitment; confident and harmonious relationships; if bolting and dragging you along, a feeling of being carried along by events or other people.

Ice If you are skating over the ice, a temporary period of stability between two periods of change; if the ice is thin or prevents you from travelling, circumstances have trapped you or you feel emotionally frozen, perhaps because of hurt or betrayal.

Infidelity If enjoying an illicit relationship, you are working through sexual inhibitions or preoccupied with more general freedom issues within your current relationship; if being betrayed or very guilty about betraying, there may be suppressed issues of trust and sexuality.

Island Withdrawal from conflict; a sanctuary from the world; if trapped on an island, a fear of solitude; if hiding from pursuers on one, a desire to escape from pressures.

Judge/jury An authority figure that can give you permission to take an action, reassure you about a course of action or absolve you from guilt; if found guilty, you may be accepting blame for others' shortcomings or judging yourself too harshly.

Jumping If leaping effortlessly over objects or even buildings, confidence, assured success and justifiable optimism; if failing to clear the objects, fear of risking failure or attempting projects that are too ambitious.

Killing/murder If committing the murder, killing off a redundant part of your life or a destructive situation; if the victim, fear of an abusive person or a situation destroying your identity.

King, queen or other royalty If a member of royalty or welcomed by them, your own self-image is high; if the royalty are dismissive or hostile, you may feel inferior to authority figures and be assuming the role of child or subject.

Ladder If climbing one, taking steps towards high ideals, ambitions and desires; if fearful of climbing or clinging to a ladder swaying in the wind, a fear of aiming high and failing.

Lift/elevator Rising above problems or to a higher level of awareness; a need to move away from familiar occupations and territory; if trapped in a lift, feeling stifled by a situation or a close relationship.

Lightning/storms A sudden awareness or insight; a cleansing of stagnant energies; movement and change; the need to learn from experience and rebuild in a new way after some form of loss.

Lions/tigers/wild animals Survival energies; awakening sexuality; the power of the hunter to seek out new opportunities; positive anger against injustice and inertia; becoming overwhelmed by negative feelings, especially when another person is mentally cruel or cold.

Magician/wizard Creative power, ingenuity and an awareness of the world of the spirit; if your inner magician, inspiration or a creative solution; if the trickster aspect, the temptation to take the easy path or one that involves wheeling and dealing.

Missing items/people If losing a broken item, a burden or a childhood toy, casting off obstacles to change and progress; if losing a job or a lover, hidden doubts about them; if losing something essential, a deep-seated fear of loss of love or security or a part of yourself.

Mist/fog If you can pass through the mist, you may find yourself in another dimension; if coming through mist into a clear landscape, the resolution of long-standing uncertainty; if lost in fog, especially if you are driving, concerns about a decision and the need for impartial advice.

Money If inheriting or winning money, either wish-fulfilment or that money-making opportunities are around you; if losing money or being overwhelmed by demands for it, either financial problems in your daily world or low energy levels.

Monsters Confronting fears from the past and defeating them; if hiding or running from them, destructive feelings may be unnecessarily distorting present reactions; possible dislike of self caused by early negative reactions by parents or teachers.

Mother If you are the mother, love, fertility, creativity and the ability to make others happy; if your own mother or an ideal maternal figure, healing and empowerment; if a sad mothering experience, a need to ask for support in your daily life and nurture yourself more.

Nakedness If your nakedness is giving you pride and pleasure, confirmation that you are not afraid to show your true self or express your inner needs; if naked in a public place and feeling ashamed or being ridiculed, the feeling that you are only acceptable by remaining in the background.

Ocean/flowing water Deep emotions that offer new levels of commitment and intimacy, spiritual development and enhanced psychic power; possible travel overseas or opportunities connected with far-off places; if you are tossed in a small boat on a stormy ocean, intense emotional pressure by others; if engulfed by a tidal wave, desire and fear of major changes, but you will survive.

Orphan If abandoned in a harsh world, unresolved sorrows and loss from childhood or a sense of being alone in the present; also a sense of loss if younger family members have left home; if rescuing an orphan, the rediscovery of an abandoned project or talent.

Prison/cage Recognition that instinctive reactions and emotions need to be temporarily restrained; the inability to speak or act freely in a relationship; being bound by compulsions, addictions and obsessions.

Quarrel If winning a quarrel, the successful clearing of stagnation and past resentments; losing or becoming upset, the desire but inability to disagree with an authority figure or someone close.

Rape/sexual attack Cleansing of remaining trauma from actual abuse; deep-seated anger at loss of power or mental abuse in a relationship; the need to talk through fears of sexuality.

Rodents such as rats or mice Possible eating away of inertia and stagnation, but also a feeling of being attacked on many fronts by issues that cannot be ignored and seem to multiply by the day.

Snake Shedding the redundant; fertility; both the mysteries of the Mother Goddess and male phallic potency; the shadow self.

Swarming insects A need to join with others and to persevere to overcome a seemingly immovable object or organisation; if ants are swarming over food or the house, a fear of being overwhelmed by small matters.

Teeth The ability to live life to the full, assertiveness and action; if falling out, not only problems with teeth and gums, but fears of seizing an opportunity or holding on to a relationship; if a smile is malevolent, a warning about the smiler.

Telephone Important urgent communication, from either the unconscious or a person who has not been in touch for a while;

frequently communication will follow soon; if unable to get through or hear the speaker, frustration at being unable to communicate something important and/or hear your inner voice.

Travel If a good journey, a good augury for the days ahead; if through lovely scenery, a harmonious current life path; also a desire to travel; if there are problems with transport, fears that plans will go awry or of being railroaded into situations beyond your control (*see also* Flying and Ocean).

Visitors If welcome but unexpected, the arrival of news; if visitors from the past, desire for the renewal of old friendships or an indication that present friendships need attention; if unwelcome, intrusions into personal space or time.

Appendix II

Deities of the Night

Here is a summary of the gods and goddesses I have mentioned, as well as others you can use as a focus for ritual and meditation. You can also find many more. I would suggest you choose three or four with whom you have an affinity and collect information about them. You will add to this knowledge as you meet them in ritual, visualisation work and dreams.

Crone Goddesses

Badhbh/Nemhain One of the triple Crone sisters of the Morrigu, the Irish battle goddesses; she appeared as a raven or a wolf on the battlefield and would herald the end of time when her Otherworld cauldron overflowed. Invoke her for increasing your prophetic powers, for accepting what cannot be changed and for issues of mortality.

The Cailleach The Celtic Triple Goddess in her winter aspect. She created the landscape, casting stones from her basket as she flew through the sky to form mountain ranges. Invoke her for all winter rituals, for embracing the unknown and for working with the ebbs and flows of the year.

Grandmother Spider The Native North American Crone who

wove the web of the world and taught wisdom, healing and crafts and protected infants from bad dreams with her dream catchers. Invoke her for peaceful sleep, banishing children's nightmares, preserving tradition and rebuilding relationships or your life.

Hecate Crone goddess, daughter of Tartarus, the original Underworld god, and Nyx or Night, the daughter of Chaos. Originally held power over the heavens, Earth and the Underworld, but with the rise of Zeus was banished to the sad, dark abode of lost souls and wandering ghosts. Invoke her for inner journeys and work with the shadow self, as well as protection in dark and lonely places.

Lunar Deities

Alako The Romany Moon god, guardian of children and of married couples, who took the souls of the dead to the Moon. Ceremonies in his honour were performed at the full Moon. Invoke him for family affairs, for wedded bliss and for all rites of passage. Use him for divination at the time of the full Moon.

Aningan The Inuit Moon god and brother of Seqinek, the Sun goddess, whom he was constantly chasing through the sky. A great hunter with a sledge loaded with seal skins and a team of spotted dogs who occasionally chased their prey down to Earth, where they were seen as shooting stars. Invoke him in full Moon magic for change, for abundance and for striving after spiritual illumination and seemingly impossible goals.

Ariadne A form of the Cretan Moon goddess Briomartis, who was also an ancient serpent and fate deity. Her oracular priestesses used baskets of snakes in divination. Statues show Ariadne's arms likewise wreathed with serpents. Invoke her for fertility, in divination, for unconscious wisdom, prophecy and hidden powers.

Artemis Greek goddess of the waxing Moon and virgin huntress, twin sister of Apollo, to whom she acted as midwife; associated with safe childbirth and the protection of animal mothers and their young. Invoke her in outdoor rituals, especially woodland ones, and for goals needing courage and action.

Bast/Bastet The cat-headed ancient Egyptian Moon goddess, deity of fertility, healing and protection, especially of pregnant women and those in childbirth, who protected the Sun god Ra every night by fighting the evil serpent Apep. Invoke her for fertility, in pregnancy and labour, for healing, shapeshifting, night-time cat rituals and protection.

Blodeuwedd The Celtic Welsh maiden aspect of the Triple Goddess, deity of May Day, of the waxing Moon and the blossoming Earth, created from nine kinds of flowers to be the bride of the young god of light, in her most ancient form the ninefold goddess of the Isles of the Blest, the Celtic Otherworld, also an owl goddess. Invoke her for rituals of the waxing Moon, for women's mysteries, for wisdom and prophecy and for all kinds of night magic.

Cerridwen The Welsh full Moon goddess and keeper of the cauldron of inspiration, mistress of shapeshifting and prophecy, goddess of Druidic initiation and of creativity, ruler of decay, death and rebirth. Invoke her in shapeshifting for overcoming fears of losing your identity or ceasing to exist, for prophecy and for healing herb craft.

Diana The Graeco-Roman Moon goddess, huntress and Queen of the Witches, originally associated with the waxing Moon; in Roman times became goddess of all aspects of the Moon and deity of healing wells, especially those linked to fertility rites. Invoke her just before dawn for sacred well ceremonies and for empowerment rituals, especially close to the full Moon, for healing and for outdoor night magic.

Isis The ancient Egyptian Moon mother goddess, Lady of Night Magic and Mistress of the Sea, whose special star was Sothis or Sirius. As Mistress of the Moon her face was veiled from those who were not initiated in her rites. Invoke her for more formal night magic, for star watching, sea rituals and all worries about mothers and children.

Luna Greek goddess of the full Moon; also the Roman Moon goddess who ruled the months and the seasons, she was especially honoured on the first day of the waning cycle. In alchemy Queen Luna was the female principle in the divine marriage with the Sun, King Sol. Invoke her for full Moon and early waning Moon magic, for needs that may take months to come to fruition and for transformation.

Selene The Greek goddess specially associated with the full Moon, sometimes forming a triplicity with Artemis and Hecate. Twin sister of Helios the Sun god and a prolific mother, who rose at night from the sea in her chariot drawn by white horses and rode high in the sky at full Moon. Invoke her for fertility, for mothering rituals and for channelling wisdom at full Moon.

Deities of Winter, Death and the Underworld

Anubis The ancient Egyptian black jackal-headed god, son of Nephthys and Osiris, who helped his mother and Isis to mummify the body of the slain Osiris and became lord of funeral rites and embalming, protecting the dead from evil spirits and accompanying them to the Halls of Judgement. Invoke him for the preservation of what is of worth, for protection and for integrity.

Morgan le Fey Goddess of death and winter, she was the daughter of the Welsh sea goddess Le Fey and half-sister of King Arthur. High priestess of the magical Isle of Avalon, she was also true sovereign of the land and was loving towards all who revered the Earth, though ruthless to those who broke her sacred trust. Invoke her for winter and sea rituals, for work at ancient sites, for protection of the Earth and for fighting against injustice and betrayal.

Nephthys Ancient Egyptian goddess of twilight, eclipses and the dark night, sister of Isis and a guardian of the dead, often depicted with a crown and dark wings, she stood at the head of a coffin with Isis at the foot, comforted the bereaved and also acted as midwife. Invoke Nephthys for protection of the very old and the very young, for rituals of endings and for help in times of spiritual or emotional darkness.

Persephone The Greek maiden goddess of transformation who was abducted by Hades and became Queen of the Underworld for the winter months, returning to the world as the light-bringer in spring. Invoke her in the autumn to mark the coming of winter and at the end of winter for the return of the light, and call on her to bring comfort to young women who have suffered loss or abuse.

Rhiannon A Welsh Moon goddess, associated with white horses, a goddess of fertility, death and the Celtic Otherworld, a bringer of prophetic dreams. Her magical blackbirds made those entering the Otherworld forget their sorrows and the passing of time. Invoke her for healing, especially through dreams, for all dream work, for making time pass faster when waiting for relief and for the return of hope.

Deities of the Night

Nott The Viking goddess of night who rode her dark chariot through the sky, drawn by her shining black horse Frost-Mane, from whose mane dropped the dew of restoration. Dellinger, god of dawn, fathered her radiant son Daeg (Day), when they united briefly at the edge of the world. Invoke her for peaceful sleep and dreams, for times when you must be awake at night or keep vigil and for using the transition between night and dawn for empowerment.

Nut The ancient Egyptian sky goddess, mother of the gods and of all living things, she arched her body over the Earth and her husband Geb, the Earth god. She was mother of Ra, the Sun god, and early myths tell how he returned to her womb every night to be reborn at dawn. Invoke her for all star and night magic, for protection of the Earth and all who live on its surface and for rituals of rebirth and regeneration.

Nyx Greek goddess of the night and death, pictured in a black star-studded robe with dark wings, she lived in a cave in the West. Each night she crossed the sky in a dark chariot pulled by black horses. She was the mother of Hypnos, god of sleep. Invoke her for psychic dreams and astral travel and for rituals at midnight or when it is a moonless night.

Appendix III

Angels of the Night and Winter

When angelology became popular in medieval times, specific angels were linked to the weather and the seasons. The angelic rank known as Virtues were believed to be responsible for the natural elements and the ordering of the seasons. Information is quite scant and scattered about some of these seasonal guardian angels, but you can focus on the angel name and allow images to form.

The Archangel Michael, though Archangel of the Sun, is identified as the supreme ruler of inclement weather such as snow, rain and hail.

The best way to get in touch with these powerful but helpful angels is to stand in a rainstorm or experience raw winter days. In a hot climate you can visualise them at cooler times of the day and year, as their powers are ones we all need. As earlier, I have referred to the angels as 'he', but you can visualise them as male or female.

Angels of the Dark Times of the Year

Cambriel or Cabriel The angel of January (with the Archangel Gabriel), he is one of the six angels who ruled over the four regions of heaven. Visualise him as a sphere of light illuminating the darkness, a shimmering presence that melts the snows and ice and leaves no footprint. Invoke him for illumination in the dark days of winter, for the reawakening of feelings after betrayal or loss and for making plans that can be realised in the spring.

Barchiel or Barakiel The Archangel of February and called the lightning of God, he is one of the four rulers of the Seraphim and in a number of traditions one of the seven great Archangels. Visualise him in rich dark robes of red and gold, with forked lightning shooting from his halo, surrounded by a field of sparks. Invoke him for matters of speculation or taking a chance, but most of all for breaking through barriers, material and spiritual, and for sudden insights.

Barbiel The angel of October and the ninth day of the Moon, its waxing cycle and a prince of Virtues. Later regarded as a fallen angel, he protects the dead. Visualise him in robes coloured like autumn leaves and with a golden brown halo that becomes brighter as the Moon increases. Invoke him for bringing matters to fruition, for abundance, for rituals at twilight during the waxing Moon and for working with our shadow side.

Adnachiel or Advachiel The angel of November, he is ruler of the lowest order of angels who commune most freely with humans. He is a very approachable angel and can be seen on foggy days even during dim daylight, helping those who have lost their way physically and spiritually. Visualise his brightness like that of the Sun on a winter's day, shining suddenly through mist and bringing warmth and light. Invoke him for letting go of what is not needed, for welcoming the winter, for getting back on track and for enjoying every unexpected moment of brightness.

Anael or Hanael The Archangel of December, Anael is the ruling angel of Principalities, the rank above Archangels, who are the guardians of continents and administer global affairs. He took the prophet Enoch to heaven. A ruler of Venus and also one of the Archangels of the Moon, he carries prayers upwards to the higher heavens. Visualise him in deep green with a globe of the world, striving to lead mortals towards peace and to respect the environment. Invoke him for all green matters, for reconciliation, for all who are vulnerable and for help with relationships.

Angels of the Dark Seasons

Attarib/Altarib The angel of winter, he offers protection against the season's hardships and dearth. He orders the transition of the year and the return of the light. Visualise him with a halo of ice, surrounded by cold winds and flurries of snow, the old father of winter whose tiny lantern you may follow to warmth and shelter. Invoke him for an easy winter, physically and emotionally, for protection against financial and material hardship, and for rest and the chance to develop your inner world of dreams.

Torquaret The angel of autumn, he is celebrated at the harvest. He is a reaper angel and so is associated with justice. Visualise him in a russet robe with deep orange wings, surrounded by fruits and vegetables and the last of the corn. Invoke him for all matters of justice, for self-assessment, and for asking for what you need and in return offering your finest gifts for the good of others.

Angels of Inclement Weather

Charoum Angel of the North (with the Archangel Uriel), the direction of the winter and of midnight, he was traditionally invoked for protection against the fiercest of the winter weather.

Oertha Another angel of the North who has a flaming torch that he holds to stop his own great power freezing the world.

Visualise either angel shimmering with ice and icicles for a halo, exuding not cold but 'fire ice' that blazes with inner light. Invoke them against North winds and all inclement weather, for courage and for the power to blow away what is decaying or destructive.

Matariel, Ridya and Zalbesael Angels of the rains who have recently become linked to drought and the need for clean water, as well as protection against flood damage. Traditionally, to bring rain you chant their names continuously (in the above order) while scattering clockwise circles of sacred water over a dry or polluted area. To take away rain, cast anti-clockwise and reverse the order of the names as you scatter your sacred water, ending with 'if it is right to be'. Visualise these angels constantly moving in robes of grey and blue, their dark grey wings shedding raindrops. Invoke them for bringing rain to dry regions, for protecting water sources, for guarding against floods and for releasing stagnation in your life.

Raguel The angel of ice and snow, Raguel is ever vigilant to make sure the other angels maintain their purity and it is said he will bring forth the lesser angels of ice and snow against the unrighteous at the Last Judgement, though the eighth-century Church Fathers thought him a fallen angel. Far-seeing, he holds intentions to be as significant as deeds. Visualise him in dark grey and silver robes with a halo flashing with icicles, with all-penetrating ice-blue eyes and a sword of fire. Invoke him for protection against malice and spite, for personal integrity and for developing a sense of wise judgement.

Ramiel Angel of thunder and endower of prophetic visions, Ramiel guards the sixth heaven, where the Cherubim live and angels study the seasons, and is one of the seven main Archangels in a number of systems. An Archangel of mercy, he will lead the faithful into heaven after Michael has weighed their souls. Ramiel also brings visions. He was later unfairly regarded as a fallen angel. Visualise him sweeping, grey, black and magnificent, across the skies, but also making sure that animals and people have shelter from the storm. Listen to his wise words as the thunder rolls. Invoke him for increasing clairvoyant and prophetic powers, for all matters of fidelity and trust and for shelter against emotional as well as actual storms.

Angels of Darkness

Aftiel The angel of twilight, Aftiel is a shadowy angel, best seen outdoors as the final rays of the Sun are dying, especially near ancient places that have been Christianised, such as cathedrals and holy wells. His comforting words are whispered on the wind. Visualise him in grey semi-transparent robes with silvery grey wings and a halo containing the last purple rays of sunlight. Invoke him for protection at night and in lonely places, for letting go of the tensions and mistakes of the day, and for all who have no homes to go to.

Jeduthun Leading angel of the evening choirs in heaven, originally he was a mortal musician, famed in the Psalms for praising God, and was elevated to the ranks of angels, whom he leads in singing at twilight. Visualise him with his scrolls of music in the evening light, a faint rainbow formed from the harmony of the notes around his head. Invoke him for protection when you feel neglected, for all creative ventures, for seeking what is of spiritual worth and for bringing grace and harmony into your world.

Leliel/Lailah Angel of the night, Leliel also protects the spirits of infants at birth and is said to have helped Abraham. Like other Dark Angels, he became associated unfairly with evil, but brings quiet dreams and guards against night terrors and psychic attack. Visualise him in dark robes with stars for a halo, enfolding his soft grey feathery wings around you when your mind is racing in the night. Invoke him against insomnia and nightmares and for protection at night.

Angels of the Moon and Stars

Angels of the Moon There are many angels associated with the Moon, one for each day of its cycle. Of these, Ofaniel and Abuzohar are most often invoked in magic, on Monday, the Moon's own day. Like Gabriel, Archangel of the Moon, they are most potent in the third hour after sunset on a Monday. Visualise your Moon angel in silver with an aura of moonbeams and a crescent Moon for a halo. Invoke him for all Moon rituals, for banishing fears when the Moon cannot be seen and for developing your spiritual side.

Zikiel/Ziquiel The angel of comets and meteors, Zikiel is also an angel of lightning and shooting stars and so is best seen at around 3 a.m. He will appear as a flash of brilliance in the darkness and his halo will emanate sparks in all directions. Visualise him bathed in gentle starlight, in pearl grey robes, with pearl wings that in a second can radiate dancing light that will fall to Earth. Invoke Zikiel for all star magic, for a burst of inspiration or illumination and as a catalyst for change.